CLOSER
TO
Poetry & Prose from
Maximum Security
FREEDOM

Edited by Chris Belden

CLOSER
TO
FREEDOM

Poetry & Prose from Maximum Security

Edited by Chris Belden

woodhall press
Woodhall Press | Norwalk, CT

woodhall press

Woodhall Press, 81 Old Saugatuck Road, Norwalk, CT 06855
WoodhallPress.com

Cover design: Danny Meoño
Layout artist: L.J. Mucci

Library of Congress Cataloging-in-Publication Data available

ISBN 978-1-954907-74-4   (paper: alk paper)
ISBN 978-1-954907-75-1   (electronic)

First Edition
Distributed by Independent Publishers Group
(800) 888-4741

Printed in the United States of America

A solitary boulder
Stands at the border,
And I climb atop it.

Up above, here, I can see for miles all around.
Up above, I am closer to freedom.
I will stay here until I die.

— "In Memoriam" by Ian T. Cooke

Contents

Preface..1

Introduction 3

Isschar M. Howard 14

Mashawn Gr▨ne..22

Lucky Barbera 26

Patrick Walsh 28

Ronald Bey...38

L▨ Brewer...42

Abdullah As Siddiq 44

Real Rell...48

Marquis Jackson...49

Juan Botello..61

Norman Gaines 62

J.V. Harvey...68

José Luis Pesante, Jr...70

Nathaniel Boykin 77

The Doves 79

Christopher T. Berchem..80

Martin P. Gingras 85

Charles Logan 88

Mount Yeti 89

Kylie Brewer...93

Felipe Colón (aka C▨-Lo)...94

Latone James...98

John Brewer III 100

Ivan Diaz..106

David Kendrick...108

Anthony Brunetti...112

Danyell Pickett...115

Michael Streater...116

Ian T. Cooke 124

Mystery...142

Nathaniel O. Chambers 143

Terrance D. Thompson 152

Rash█n Giraud 156
Rocky Williams, aka The Illestrator 159
Charles Devorce 165
Alexis "Lex" Melendez 167
Kenneth Anderson 182
Jamar Boyd 188
Chauncey Watts 190
D. Paschal, aka K. L. Paschal-Barros 197
Lawrence Perry 198
Robert (Moët) Coover 205
Solomon Boyd 207
Exodus Cooke 221
Quan A. Soyini... 227
Max Well... 229
Andy M.T 234
Akhivelli 238
Chey-Patron 253
Israel 257
Stylus 262
Veronica-May Clark... 266
John-Russell Bossé 280
Keith Ellis... 286
Michael P. Mark, Jr. 289
John L. Benjamin.. 292
Hunter McGinty 295
Kar█m Leach 299
Jenkins Tarlue 300
Bryan Goodwin... 302
Tall Eagle 305
Joseph Grosso 310
Vaughn Walker (aka Legend)... 316

Contributor Bios 323
Acknowledgments 339
About the Editor 340

Preface

From 2009 to 2020, I led a weekly creative writing workshop at Garner Correctional Institution, a maximum-security prison in Connecticut. Over those years, I edited and published nine issues of the literary magazine *Sentences* to showcase the amazing prose and poetry being produced by the writers in the workshop. The magazine was distributed mostly within the prison itself, though I also made copies available to those on the outside who were curious about what kind of work these writers were capable of. Most of the writings contained in *Closer to Freedom* have been culled from those nine publications.

People have asked why I chose to enter a prison week after week in order to help convicted prisoners with their writing. My answer: having led and participated in workshops for many years, I had witnessed the healing power of writing, and few in this world require more healing than the incarcerated. Presented with an alternative method of channeling their energy and feelings, these budding writers have produced impressive and often beautiful works of art. On a more practical level, multiple studies have shown that education opportunities reduce the recidivism rate of those recently released from prison. Having spoken to many formerly incarcerated individuals, I am happy to report that they credit their time in our workshop as helping them to cope with the challenges of incarceration—and the challenges of freedom.

After the COVID-19 pandemic shut down prison volunteer programs in March 2020, I missed visiting the writers but was able to get my "fix" by poring through every issue of *Sentences*, editing and rearranging the poems, stories, and essays, and reaching out to the authors (via the good old U.S. Mail) for permission to publish their pieces in book form. While too many remain behind bars, I was happy to find that several of my former students are now living outside prison walls, working and contributing to their communities and families.

I did my best to feature everyone who agreed to appear in these pages, but the reader will notice that some authors are represented more than others. This is not due to the quality (or lack thereof) of their writing, but to the fact that some writers attended the workshop longer, some were more willing to share their work with me, and some were simply more prolific. A few, unfortunately, were unwilling, or unable, to grant permission.

Early on in my tenure at Garner C.I., one of my students described why he enjoyed his visits to the prison library and the writing workshop held there. "It's like we're free for a couple of hours," he told me. This collection represents the many hours we spent writing and talking about writing, as well as the hours spent alone in six-by-nine cells with a pen and a notebook, conjuring the words needed to express otherwise untapped feelings—in other words, the hours spent "closer to freedom."

Chris Belden

INTRODUCTION:
How to Teach Writing in Prison
By Chris Belden

"I died in 1960 from a prison sentence and poetry brought me back to life."
-Etheridge Knight

1
Follow the rules of the institution.

Before each weekly workshop session, store your valuables and any unauthorized items in the locker provided. Remove any metal objects, including your belt and wristwatch, before passing through the metal detector. If female, remember not to wear inappropriate clothing: short shorts, short skirts, revealing tops, etc. Do not wear clothing that is too ostentatious, i.e., clothing that implies you might be wealthy. Do not wear long necklaces, lanyards, or other objects that could be used to injure you. No electronic devices—cell phones, cameras, recorders of any kind—are permitted. Make sure to bring two forms of ID, one to exchange for a locker key, another to exchange for a visitor pass from the corrections officer (CO) behind a thick plate of bulletproof glass.

Before you enter the prison interior, a CO may or may not ask to inspect your notebook. Every corrections officer is different, displaying varying degrees of allegiance to the rules. For example, even though you've regularly arrived with stapled pages—copies of poems you intend to hand out, or samples of the students' work you've typed up—the CO might ask you to remove all the staples. While you pry the little metal pieces from the paper with your fingers, this more cautious CO will explain that an inmate could use a staple as a weapon.

2
Always be a little afraid.

When your CO escort arrives, follow him through the sally port, an enclosed space between two heavy doors, both of which can never be opened at the same time. Try not to jump out of your skin when the second door slams shut with a loud clang. As you follow the escort up a set of stairs and down a long antiseptic hallway, you might make small talk, but don't mention that the place seems quiet today. "We don't like to use that word in here," he'll say with a frown. "It's bad luck."

He may then ask what you do here, and when you tell him you teach a writing workshop he'll say, "You volunteer for that? *Why?*" From the way he says this, you know you won't be able to convince him, in the few moments you have, that a writing class can change people's lives, so simply tell him that you find the class interesting. He will then make it clear that he does not find the men he guards at all interesting, and that if you spent enough time with them, like he has, you'd recognize that they're all "playing games." This will remind you of the warning given at orientation that prison inmates are "keen judges of character and superb con artists." That, and the constant threat of physical harm—COs are outnumbered and, in some cases, out-weaponed—would eventually grow calluses on anyone's empathy. So just nod and acknowledge that your escort is probably right.

Follow him past the kitchen area, where the smell of fried food greases the air, and down another long hallway. On the right, through several large plate glass windows, you'll see a group of men assembled in the library for the workshop. They're all dressed in identical uniforms, tan tops and trousers that resemble hospital scrubs. Some of the men will see you and wave hello. Many will sit chatting in the chairs that have been arranged in a semicircle. A few will sit quietly, alone with their thoughts.

4

Make sure to thank your escort before you enter the library. You will not be guarded for the next few hours, and, even though you may come to believe that your status as a volunteer teacher grants you some protection, you want to be on good terms with the COs. From here on in, the only security between you and a group of convicted felons will be a librarian wearing a body alarm—a red buttoned device on his belt that, when pressed, alerts the officers to come to your aid. So say thanks, and as you enter the library, remember this other bit of advice from orientation: in case of a violent or potentially violent situation, stand with your back against the nearest wall. And: in case of a hostage situation, remain calm and do what is asked of you.

3
Expect the unexpected.

Upon your arrival, Mark Aldrich will open the locked door. Mark is a bit disheveled in the way of artists and writers, which is what he is when he's not performing the dry duties of a prison librarian. Observe him closely. Under Mark, the library is an oasis where the incarcerated quench their thirst for knowledge, creativity, and intellectual stimulation, and he will show you how to treat even the most disreputable people humanely without coddling them.

Depending on how long it has taken you to get through the security gauntlet, it might now be anywhere from 8:30 to 8:45 a.m. The workshop will typically get started around nine. For the next fifteen minutes or so, your students will straggle into the library and sign in. They must be on an official list for the class, and if the COs in charge of letting them out of their cells are not in a generous mood, some men may run late or not show up at all. Others may arrive late because they first need to visit the nurse's office, where they receive their daily meds. A number of inmates may miss the workshop altogether because of a lockdown in one or more cell blocks. Perhaps one of them was stabbed in the eye in the cafeteria this morning because he took too many containers of milk, which means all the students from cell block E will not be in the workshop today.

Every week, it seems, there will be an inmate who just doesn't want to rise from his bunk, even to experience the relative freedom of the library.

The good news is that most of these guys will want to be here. The workshop is not mandatory, and no credit is given aside from a certificate that may help a little in a probation hearing. (If a "playing games" inmate is there just for this certificate—if he has no interest in writing but just wants the little gold star on his record—it will become very clear very fast: "Do I get a certificate for this?" will be his first question. "When do I get my certificate?" will be his last. In between, he'll do very little writing.) The men will have been vetted by Mark, who gets to know them during their weekly visits to the library, chats with them about books and other topics, and susses out who might be interested in writing. Which doesn't mean that a lot of guys won't drop out along the way during the eight-session term. On the first day, thirty-five people might show up. By the eighth session, eight or ten might remain. Some will disappear because they can't take the heat. Some—including your favorites—will be transferred to other facilities, often without warning. *Poof*, they're gone.

4

Always work within the boundaries of your specified assignment.

After you've volunteered here for a while—maybe a few months, or at least long enough to demonstrate that this is not a lark, that you actually give a damn—some of the men will greet you warmly and shake your hand as they enter the library. They'll ask you how you're doing, and when you return the question, they'll shrug and say they're hanging in there. If Mr. K., a twenty-nine-year-old inmate who looks twenty-one, remarks, "It must be nice to be free," tell him that it *is* nice, and that when he gets out—in seven years—he needs to *stay* out. He will nod and say, "Oh, I'm never coming back *here*." (A few years later, Mr. K. will leap to his death from the upper walkway in his cell block.)

Always refer to the inmates as "Mr. So-and-So." It shows you respect them, and respect is currency in this place. By the same token, introduce yourself to them as "Mr. Belden." (By the way, never use an inmate's full name in a published essay. If a crime victim sees an assailant's name in a publication, the Department of Corrections may come under fire.)

As you work the room, some inmates might ask you about your new Nikes. "Where'd you get those, Mr. B.? How much did you pay?" When you tell them you got the shoes at Kohl's, for about fifty bucks, they'll say, "Damn! Those cost $70 in the commissary." Shoes, the rare article of clothing that is not uniform in this place, take on even greater meaning than they do on the outside. But because the inmates must purchase them—with money earned from their low-paying prison jobs—not everyone can get the kicks they'd prefer. Some guys wear deluxe basketball shoes, as white as paper because of the lack of exposure to the elements. Some guys wear modest sneakers, some wear thick leather work boots, and some wear espadrilles. You'll see at least one fellow in bedroom slippers. Family members and friends used to be allowed to send shoes in the mail, but not anymore. "The state don't make any money on the markup," the inmates will explain.

Right about now, as you continue to exchange pleasantries with the men, you might be tempted to ask a particular inmate why he's here. Some of these guys are so intelligent, and seem so reasonable, you can't imagine them committing a felony. But just as you're not to volunteer personal information about yourself, you must not inquire of anyone else's personal information, no matter how curious

7

you may be. When someone blurts out details of his case during conversation—and it will happen—you'll see how it can color your perceptions. That sensitive, intelligent fellow who does yoga was convicted of murdering a woman and will probably spend the rest of his days in prison. This toxic knowledge will now be in the air every time you speak with him.

5
Establish a routine.

At nine o'clock or so, the men will take their seats facing a podium that is actually a stand for a large dictionary and must be propped up on an overturned cardboard box to reach the necessary height. Occasionally, someone will ask to make an announcement. For example, Mr. J. might broadcast that someone has stolen the library tape dispenser. "Please return it," he'll say. "Mr. A. has done so much for all of us. Stealing library property may endanger programs like this one. Thank you very much." Or maybe Mr. W. will want to apologize to the group for some previous bad behavior and thank you for providing him an opportunity to be creative. (Don't be too shocked, though, when you're told the following week that he is in segregation—solitary confinement—for fighting.)

At this point, you should say a few words about the previous week's assignment, ask if there were any problems, and answer whatever questions they might have. Point of view is a common issue. "What's the difference between first and third person?" "If I have a character that says to another guy, 'I hate you,' does that make it first person because I used the word 'I'?" That kind of thing. Be patient. Acknowledge that writing is hard. If you have an anecdote about how hard writing is, share it. Remember E. B. White: "Writing is hard work and bad for the health."

Once these issues are resolved, step aside and ask who wants to share their work. Unlike in most workshops, someone will always be eager to go first. There is no shortage of extroverts in prison. But someone else will always need coaxing. It will feel exceedingly strange to try to talk a murderer into doing something he doesn't want to do. He may glare menacingly as you encourage him to share. He will then sigh, grumble, walk purposely slowly to the podium. He will rush the words, pause at every other line, stare at the paper in his hands. Next week he might do the same thing, but the following week he'll walk a little quicker to the podium and read more smoothly. By the end of the term, he may be one of the guys who demands to go first.

There will always be someone who has not done the assignment, either because he was too busy dealing with legal issues (filing motions, meeting with lawyers, etc.) or because he just never got around to it. Sometimes the technical elements of the assignment will be too perplexing ("Iambic *what*?"), but once in a while the assignment might prove too challenging for more personal reasons. For example, if you ask the men to write a story about themselves accomplishing a goal after being released from prison, one of your students might confess that, because he's been sentenced to 130 years, he simply could not bring himself to write about freedom. This will be one of those assignments that make you wonder if you've screwed up. It'll happen more than once. If you ask the inmates in December to write a Christmas story, one of your best, most talented students may refuse to write anything because it makes him miss his family too much. If you have them write a detailed description of waking up in their cells, a few inmates might balk at first, and one man may raise his hand and ask if you've ever been in prison. "What you're asking us to do is no joke," he'll say. "You could never know what it feels like to wake up in a six-by-nine unless you've done it yourself."

9

But in all these cases some inmates will return the following week with amazing pieces full of startling details and sensory observations. Their Christmas stories will turn out to be moving and generous:

> Despite everything going on in your everyday life, today is the day you try to focus your attention on the foster care community, where for the last five years you've been donating money and toys to kids without fathers. You're ruthless, but you know how it feels to wake up on Christmas morning without gifts. (Latone James)

The after-prison assignment will produce stories about success, romance, and family reunion:

> He pulls up to his babymother's house and sees his son sitting on his bike in the front and talking to his cousins and uncles that are his age. He gets out of the car and smiles to himself as he reads his son's lips: "Is that my daddy?" He closes the car door, and his heart softens as his son jumps off his bike and runs toward him and says, "What up, Dad?" "Everything, baby boy. Everything." (Bernard Scott)

The prison cell exercise will inspire heartbreaking howls of pain:

> I am from a cell, a toilet, a sink, a desk, a double bunk—all in one space; From a place that never should have saw my face. (Mashawn Green)

For every inmate who cannot bring himself to confront his feelings of loss and pain and fear, there will be several who jump in and produce stories that inspire and entertain.

6
Establish clear boundaries.

Invariably, a writer will ignore the "no profanity/no sex/no violence in your writing" rule that you and Mark established on day one. This means you'll have to shut down the inmate reading his story about a man who fantasizes about killing his girlfriend while they have sex on a beach, even though it's actually the best-written story of the week. Then expect the following:

"But it ain't creative writing if we can't write whatever the [profanity] we want!"

"We're just trying to speak the [profanity] truth!"

"This is [profanity] censorship!"

If you're lucky, one of the veterans of the workshop will pipe up at this point to defend the rule. "I used to think that way," he might say, "but remember: this is a 'creative' writing class, and sometimes you need to find more creative ways to express yourself." Thank him and go on to say that we've all heard those four-letter words, there's nothing surprising about them anymore, so let's try something different. Ask them to make you see something old in a new and startling way. If that doesn't work, just say, "Them's the rules," and move on.

7
Motivate your students to develop self-esteem.

After a writer has read his non-profane work, open up the room for comments. Though the quality of the writing will vary wildly—some inmates will have read a lot of books and absorbed the basics of storytelling; many will have written stories, poems, lyrics, and even novels on their own; others will be barely literate—be very clear that you're looking for positive criticism. These are not professional writers; they are not MFA students hoping to *become* professionals.

11

They are, for the most part, newcomers to this process. Bottom line: You want them to come back next week.

Thankfully, it's very rare for an inmate to openly diss someone's work. Mostly what they'll say is that they liked it, that they could relate to it, that it spoke the truth, etc. Try to get them past these generalities. Try to get them to go deeper: What did they like about it? What do they remember from the piece, and why? Talk a lot about the importance of details, metaphor, point of view (again). At some point, especially if they've written about their real-life experiences, the conversation may turn into a rap session about growing up in the 'hood, or the indignities of prison life. Give them a while before you steer them back to the writing. Let them make the connection that their work has made them see their lives differently, perhaps more clearly, with a little bit of distance. Wait for that moment—and it will come, not every week, but regularly—when an inmate remarks, with an appreciative grin, "Man, I never thought I'd be able to do this kind of thing." Soak this up, then rein them in by asking something technical: "Can anyone tell me what tense that story was in?"

8
Appreciate what you've got.

The workshop will run until eleven, a solid two hours. Occasionally the students may appear to actually learn something technical about writing. They might see how the appropriate metaphor can deepen the meaning of a description, or how writing in third person can achieve the distance necessary to tell a story effectively. If you're lucky, they will learn something less tangible but more important. These are people with few choices in their lives, and here is an opportunity to choose what to say and how to say it. Where they once employed intimidation and violence to express themselves, they can now choose to use language, rhyme, metaphor. In an environment where vulnerability is not only discouraged but dangerous, they can safely open themselves up without fear of judgment. Just as some may find freedom through reading books, some can find it by writing.

Before the workshop ends, explain, as clearly as possible, next week's assignment. Give handouts if possible, with specific suggestions for how to complete the assignment. If it is based on an existing poem or prose piece, include it with the handout. Gauge their enthusiasm, or lack thereof, and note which assignments appear to inspire them. Follow a "heavy" exercise—one that touches on deep feelings—with something silly ("Choose a superpower and write a story about it.")

If an inmate offers his hand before signing out and leaving the library, shake it. If he thanks you for coming, tell him he's very welcome. Make sure to mention that you'll be back, because not everyone does come back.

And when Mark escorts you downstairs, through the sally port and metal detector, and after you've retrieved your wallet and keys and cell phone, and you walk out the door into the late morning air, make sure to take note of how nice it is to be free.

Originally published in Teachers & Writers Magazine.
Winner, 2013 Bechtel Prize.

ISSCHAR M. HOWARD

My New Haven Character

I am unbreakable, born forgotten,
raised under the rock you call rock bottom.
I am Isschar Howard, mispronounced Isiea,
the boy with colored eyes, the white boy, the banana man, the albino.
I am bad, troublesome, always into something,
the boy Chee-Chee took in 'cause Etta didn't want him.
I am him—from the tribe but lives on Bristol St.,
jumped everyday by the same boys he goes to school with,
but still cool with.
See, the school, it's in the middle of the projects; in the back
used to be the high-rises filled with rats the size of cats.
Up Dixwell to Broadway, sagging pants and bandannas,
trespassing on Yale campus,
from Wexler Elementary to Helen Grant, the house I spent my summers,
Southeast Drive I got my first job as a runner.
From DCYS to DCF, an adopted product of my environment
—who am I? A menace to society,
a master, a beast, a murderer,
trapped into an emotional world of confusion,
and I'm losing.
I'm a drug addict, an alcoholic, exhausted but still clawing
toward dreams of becoming
meaningful and redeemable for what truly matters,
'cause a man's bad decision doesn't define his character.

Untitled

I miss my mother's love, her support, her guidance, her attitude, and even her discipline.

I miss her voice, her words, her wisdom.

Her ears: when I had something to say, she listened. Her whipping I hated, but I miss the purpose. I couldn't escape my past, but she encouraged me to move on. See, I was confused. My blood claimed they loved and missed me, but I couldn't understand—if you miss me so damn much, then come get me. My confusion transforms to rage, causing Mommy to hit. She says she's sorry, but I don't believe her. "When I get older I'm running away so I don't have to be with her." And I did, as a kid—headed nowhere fast. A hard head makes a soft ass, and mine is rock solid. You never realize what you have until you have to live without it. The only mother that ever loved me, I left broken-hearted. When I asked you why she didn't want me, you had no answer, so I searched for it 'cause I couldn't do without it. Thirty years later you can't love what you don't acknowledge.

I can still taste the seasoning from your fried chicken, and I can still smell the Jheri curl activator that kept your hair glistening. It hurts to know I miss what I don't have to be missing.

Scent of Life

PCP mixed with izm pollutes my system
Sippin' on a milkshake to clear my vision
Listening to the words but there's something missing
There's no meaning, am I dreaming?
"Boy, wake up!" somebody's screaming
"Her water broke—she's having the baby"
I'm in the back seat looking at my brother like he's crazy
Mob Deep bangin' out the speakers
I rubbed Blue Nile on my clothes to cover up the reefer
"The next time I catch you high, I'm leaving ya"—so said Tameika
My pregnant girlfriend, with Black, Greek, and Portuguese features
Her grandfather's a preacher and he's always preachin'
The ol' "Get right with God and you'll beat the odds"
But I believe if I don't stack the cards there's a chance I might starve
And that's a chance I can't take
I got a baby on the way so I can't break
The cold January air hits my face, today's real
I make my way to the entrance of St. Rafael's
The butterflies in my stomach is so intense it's sickening
If I hurl it'll be my guts 'cause my stomach is empty
In the waiting room it's no friends, it's family

Her cousins Booby, Smoochie, and my baby mom's mother Sandy
Waving her finger in my face, "Boy, you best not be high"
I looked her dead in her eye and told her a bold-faced lie
And she's staring me down like she wants to ring my neck
I'm like 16 years old, what you expect?
We made our way in the room where she was giving labor
My eyes watered with her pain, I wished that I could save her
Gave her my hand and she squeezed as if life depended on

Me holding on so God wouldn't send her home
A couple names she called me I don't care to share
But to be honest it felt decent for me to be there
Her squeezing turned to nails digging in my flesh
The nurse telling her to take deep breaths
Her face a mess combined with tears and sweat
And at that moment I realized how much I loved her
And how honored I was for her to be my first child's mother
The doctor tells her to push and she grunts and moans
She's in the most extreme pain, I can tell by her tone
The doctor stands in between her legs
"Keep pushing, Tameika, I can see the head"
I let her hand go to get a better view
There was a *splat* sound and out the baby flew
The doctor bobbled and cradled it in his arms
The piercing sounds of her cries were like a fire alarm
"It's a girl!" he yelled, my mouth fell to the floor
and this fool talking about do I wanna cut the umbilical cord . . .

They washed her up and placed her in Tameika's arms. I thought at that divine moment, I took part in creating a life, a bloodline that would go on forever. When I was a kid, I hated the smell of hospitals 'cause to me it was the scent of death. But, at that moment, this pale, precious little girl gave off the scent of life.

Check Out My Melody

"Nobody wanted you. Your father didn't want you. Your mother didn't want you. I took you in cause I wanted to, not cause I had to. Nobody sends me money for you."

These words, mixed with her emotions. No matter how many times I heard them, still they sent vibrations through my heart, earthquakes though my soul.

She's beautiful. She has Indian features, her skin complexion is a smooth shade of caramel. Her eyes are dark brown, and her teeth as white as pearls (maybe my teeth would be that white if I could take them out and soak them in a cup). Her dark curly hair glistens from spraying the yellow bottle of Jheri curl activator on it. Her gold bracelets, when she swings her arms, makes music. I know the melody very well.

I believe I was eight or nine years old when I talked back to my mother. "Stop hitting me!" I screamed. Her eyes got wide, her nostrils flared, and the music played louder than ever.

"Always into something." That's one way to describe me. Oh, point blank—I was a bad kid. Children shouldn't spend their childhood asking why. Many days and many nights I spent asking why. On this particular morning I drank some eggnog. It was real good, so I drank some more. Before I knew it, I had drunk the entire gallon. Last time I did this it was with the cookie dough. Not only did the music play, she bought like six more and made me eat them. Well, she tried. Let's just say I'm the reason we had roaches.

Now here I was, trying to block the music. When she finally got tired, she said something I'll never forget: "I'm not gonna use my hands no more, cause I'm hurting myself."

A new instrument for her new melody, and she played it well.

Papa Don't Preach

When he says, "You have pretty eyes,"
Say, "So does my father."

When they invite you to a party,
Remember what I told you about experiences, and
How decisions are things you have to live by—
No one smiles your smile, and no one else feels your pain!

If they say, "Just try it, it's not a big deal,"
Say, "Nah, I'm cool with what I like doing."

It's not like I'm trying to run your life;
It's just that everything dark, I've been a part of.
I know a game when it's presented,
So it's only right that I tell you that, if you keep chasing garbage,
One day you'll end up smelling like it!

When someone is stupid enough to glorify
Any negativity I did in these streets,
You just remember:

That's why I'm not there like I should be.

Alive?

Do we exist? Does my heart beat at the rhythm of hip-hop
or does it tick-tock in silence like some fancy watch?
Was I born to be ... be ... be somebody productive, positive, better?
Like time, will my words live on forever?
Is my character measured by the goals I accomplish or what I've
been through?
Or am I like a lost verse from Ms. Holiday's "Strange Fruit"?
Do I mean what I say, but later on realize I said what I don't mean?
Am I like an oxymoron if I say things like "Life's a piece of cake—
then where's the frosting or the meaning?"
Yeah, I'm alive, like a man in a coma who's not dreaming,
like a crack-head locked up who's not fiending,
like a kleptomaniac who's not stealing.
Lately I wake up in a block half-retarded,
staring at walls with portraits by forgotten artists.
Keese said it's rubbing off
like the man who woke up with fleas 'cause he slept with dogs
Pause ...
Am I living or am I just drifting,
like a man who slips in and out of consciousness?
The trauma hits, leaving my sanity with not too many places to hide,
like a man who is not supposed to cry, this is breaking my pride.
But through it all, like Ms. Angelou's poem, I still rise
and thank God for the opportunity to survive.
So goodbye to all my pity parties, no more feeling sorry,
we're not gonna live life standing still, are we?
Do we need failure to understand the true value of success?
Or are the answers like that message in a bottle that no one ever gets?
Like that moment everybody dreams of when we're relieved of stress,
mixed emotions oppressed,

it's like an asthma attack squeezing your chest,
and at that moment when Death is breathing down your neck
you realize you've been alive all along,
and one monkey don't stop no show, you gots to keep keepin' on.
Like an entire life flashed before a dying man's eyes,
it is at the time we are at our lowest that we realize
that we are indeed alive . . .

MASHAWN GREENE

Where I'm From (I)

I am from pothole roads, bacon fat in Grandma's kitchen.
I am from a place where the youth just don't listen.
I am from piss-stained walls and trash in every direction you walk,
From bums in the hall and bodies outlined in chalk.
I am from a place where you wear your Sunday best,
Hoping you don't get it dirty because you won't forget the rest;
From broken bottles and empty dreams,
The ho's, the pimps, the cons, and the schemes.
I am from a place where twenty children, not related, but we're all family—the good ol' days.
Close to Yale, close to the Shubert, but far from being praised.
I am from my brother's shoes, passed down from Dad,
From soul food, good cooking, where nothing tastes bad.
I am from a place where bullets flying and kids dying is considered the norm,
A place with sunshine, but it's always a storm.
I'm from a place where somebody gets shot almost every day,
From shattered homes, no furniture, old carpet, where parents always pray.
I'm from a place where you don't want to go.
But guess what. That's where I'm from,
The only place I know.

Quiet

Quiet
Peaceful
Footsteps
And whispers
     Shhh   listen
Toilets flushing
Sinks running
A waterfall
In the distance
     Shhh   listen
Illuminating light
Radio waves transmitted
Hard metal surfaces
Small window
Obstructed view
     Look   nah   listen
Too many days
Away from family
Missing loved ones
Yearning for happiness
     Forever
         and
               ever
   Missing . . . freedom

A Letter to God

Dear God,

I hope that you are good in the sky. I have been good today. I have a kids' Bible and I read a lot. I just read Job. Mommy always say, "You say it '*Jobe*,'" but when she get at my brother, she always say, "You need to get a J.O.B." and that's *Job*. I spell pretty good. I like spelling in school. I think Mommy has something in her water bottle she is sipping on. She get mad and drank all the water in the bottle. She even be late for work a lot. She said she need more money because her tips are not a lot of money for nothing. She need help. And Pa Pa is sick, so all Mommy money goes to his pills. They say only you can help him. God, can you please help Pa Pa feel better? All he do is sleep. He doesn't even tell me stories anymore. I want Pa Pa to play with me. If Pa Pa feel better, Mommy will have some money. And can I have a new bike? Bye bye.

This is from Little Jimmy

Where I'm From (II)

I am from a cave filled with many lost souls. You hear that? That's the blues.
I am from a pit—no, a deep, dark pit that echoes gossip and bad news.
I am from a hate factory, as many have called it,
From barbed wire fences, surrounded by it.
I am from a cell, a toilet, a sink, a desk, a double bunk—all in one space;
From a place that never should have saw my face.
I'm from recall. I said recall—don't be late.
I'm from six a.m.—you know, breakfast and cake.
I'm from a place where you work out to relieve stress, or maybe to better your health;
From a library, a school, a church—use it to better yourself.
I am from a day to four letters (L-I-F-E).
I've seen it all.
From a place, even if it's local, still $5 a call.
I am from a place where my neighbor could be a murderer or a thief, cool or lame;
From a place where, innocent or guilty, we're all treated the same.
I am from a stench—smell that, that's a lost dream.
I am from hope, and that's because of the support from my family, my team.
They say home is where the heart is. Well, home is soon to come.
Hold up. This is where I am. This can't be where I'm from.

LUCKY BARBERA

Love on the Horizon

The stiff ocean breeze took me by surprise. Lost in a daydream, I had forgotten where I was for a moment. I tilted my head up toward the sun as I pushed the fine white sand into a mound with my bare feet. It was completely quiet except for the gentle swish of the waves as they swept over the edge of the beach.

I looked over to her, still in awe of her natural beauty. I took a deep breath, which filled my lungs. Her lush evanescence permeated the air around us. It always makes me smile how she is able to do that without a hint of effort. I asked her the same question she has heard me mutter time and again: "How did I get so lucky to have found you?" She listened intently as she always does when I speak with her. However, we both know there is no need to answer such an inane inquiry. So I turned back to the water still gently moving in and gracefully sliding out.

The two of us met when I was a child. I had just climbed down from playing in an old oak tree when we first crossed paths. From that day on we were inseparable. Our childhood friendship blossomed into a romance in my mid-teens, but I knew I was in love with her that very first afternoon. Life is never dull with her; she is always changing and moving. Sometimes she is quiet and reserved, her voice barely a whisper. Other times her screams are a booming thunderstorm. She wears her emotions on her sleeve. She can be moody at times, changing on a whim from a sunny disposition to a cloudy complexion.

Although my vision might be tinted a slight shade of rose, I admit that as remarkable and unique as she is, she reacts like most women when she feels ignored or taken advantage of. She is very vocal about these sorts of slights. So, as with any delicate being, I treat her with only love and admiration. It is the best I can do for her; after all, she has shown me the most beautiful things life has to offer. Moreover, she loves me for who I am; she does not want me to change. She just wants me to protect her, and that is the way it should be. For she is Mother Nature.

PATRICK WALSH

Penny Loafers at Five

Mommy let me outside to play on a warm, bright sunny after-noon. It might be a weekend day, I don't know, but the air smells thick and moist, so it must be summertime. The concrete patio at the rear of the house is divided in half with glorious sunlight on one side and cool shade on the half nearest the house. The roof dormers cast jack-in-the-box shadows on the cement. The smell of fresh-cut grass tickles my nose as I gaze past our fallow yard to the lush green lawns of the neighbors, the green so full and deep in color compared to the dull yellow and brown decay of our yard. I see no one cutting the grass or enjoying the lawn on one side of us, so I turn to see the yard behind the blue house on the other side. No one is there, either. The yards of the three houses adjacent to the back are also empty. There are kids living in those houses, but I'm all alone out here. I gently kick a stone from the shadows across the cement and into the bright sunlight. The warmth of the sun comforts the bare skin of my arms and face but is also warm enough to burn if I linger too long. Raising my hand to shield my eyes I look toward the sun. My eyes blink uncontrollably as they fill with wetness. The brightness wins and my eyes wander back toward the shade for relief. Black as night, I can't see anything. Within seconds, the darkness lightens and the trashcans at the end of the patio come into view. My toe finds the small stone and skids it back into the shadows toward the cans. The shade feels cool and refreshing, my eyes are relieved from needing to squint. I notice the feet of my favorite teddy bear sticking out of the trash barrel like he had excitedly dived in to retrieve some type of delicious teddy bear treat. I feel happy, and with a giggle I bounce over to his upside-down feet. "Aw, Teddy," I mutter with glee, "Let me rescue you from the smelly garbage can." Suddenly my heart sinks as I'm filled with feelings of doom and dread. Chaos and confusion pound and pressurize my skull. Everything I'd forgotten from the night before comes rushing back to my mind. "Where is his head?" Teddy Bear's head is gone! Twisting, turning knots wave through my insides, my knees feel weak, and I begin to tremble remembering Daddy's rage the night before, screaming, "No son of mine will be a little pussy who plays with stuffed animals!" Frightful visions flash of my father tearing Teddy's head from his body. My tears taste like salt as I remember Teddy Bear's head sliding down the far wall of the living room. My ears ring like a thousand million crickets on a dark muggy night. The cool, refreshing shade now feels eerily cold as a chill shivers up my spine. Why does the air suddenly smell like the beer seeping from his pores? I'm so fiercely alone, but I feel as if someone is there watching me. My weight shifts from foot to foot and I grab the front of my shorts to resist the urge to pee. I need to hide. Quickly, I sit between the trash cans with my back to the wall. It smells sour down here. Clenching my headless bear, I shiver. It's hot outside, but I feel so cold. Huh...what's that noise? Frozen, I can't breathe, afraid to even move my eyes. Footsteps coming closer. My heart pounding in my ears so hard I can't hear. But I do hear, and it terrifies me more because I know who it is. The gravel under the soles of his feet crunches louder and louder. I'm trapped. There's nowhere to run. Closer and closer the footsteps come, and they stop, almost toe-to-toe with my feet. Opening my eyes, I'm too scared to look up. Those pennies in his loafers are bright and shiny. They look so nice, but then why does the love from his fists feel so terrifying?

Seeds of Time

If only you could see me, if only you had seen me.

If only you could see my arms are always raised upward in gratitude and thanksgiving no matter the power of the tempest, or darkness of the night.

If only you realized I've always been a part of you, inside of you, that I've been here from the beginning, before you, for you to learn from and to help you, not for you to destroy me and my relatives.

If only you didn't see yourself as superior, greater and smarter than the Creator of Life, with your delusion of controlling even the simple beauty of life.

If only you hadn't poisoned, in the name of progress and technology, the streams, the rivers, the oceans, the air, even your food...everything you touched.

If only you had appreciated the purity and cleanliness of the air you breathed and how it got that way.

If only you knew how to actually practice ethical business operations rather than just talk, and talk, and talk about such, while acting the hypocrite, pointing fingers everywhere but at yourselves.

If only you had respected each other, respected yourselves; stopped the deprivation of women in secret and laughing about it openly, stopped murdering your own offspring.

If only you had kept your children safe and let them outside to play, adhered to simple things like regular dinners with them that *you* prepared.

If only you hadn't allowed the children you sacrificed in the name of unbridled capitalism to become so desensitized to humanity and to reality.

If only you had listened to the land, heard the cry of the mountains, the flowers, the birds, and the planet when they pleaded to you over, and over, and over again.

If only you had heard their warning, then you wouldn't have felt the sickness, the suffocating, the drowning, and your skin burning as it peeled from your bones.

If only you could realize I'm the last of my kind, the last of any kind, the last known tree, standing here on the waste land of your planetary devastation. But your ears are still shut, your mouths gaped open, and your graves are full.

If only you could see me, if only you had seen me. You'd see fresh buds forming at my fingertips, and my seeds, like tears, falling to the ground.

If only...

More than a Photo

A peculiar day, in this photo with an aged tint.
The temperature appears a bit chilly, but the atmosphere warm,
our partially leaf-covered yard
isolates a small mound of snow in a corner.
Spring or fall, I question,
yet the long warm shadows cast from nearby leafless trees suggest
early snowfall, tardy leaf raking, autumn.

Half greenish-tan lawn, half orange, reddish, and brown,
fallen leaf cleanup seems to be the task.
In the background I stand, rake in hand,
facing away.

Center-framed
in the air, dead leaves linger,
frozen in time.
A little tow-headed boy they surround,
grinning ear to ear, my son, held in excitement,
the ancient joy of throwing leaves impossibly high.

Foreground left,
running through neatly raked leaves,
a little girl, my daughter,
pigtails, barrettes, arms in mid-stride,
around her head the sun's radiance glows.
Toddlers both adorable, winter coats cover
Cute, child-size OshKosh overalls.
Tee-shirt, cut-off sleeves and jeans cover me.
If a thousand words a picture's worth,
a thousand cheers this one holds.

Not visual memory alone,
warming my heart,
but with acoustics this photo sings.

Son and daughter
turned man and woman.
Tender little fingers then, adult hands now,
caring these days for their own toddlers.
Still, the sound of that peculiar day I hear
to my ears a symphony,
as I worked then,
all these years held in my soul now,
for the laughter, a grateful heart
and unconditional love,
for the high-pitched screeches saying,
"Jump in the leaves, Daddy! Daddy, let's do that again!"

On the Free-Way

Trees of many sizes and shapes blur at 65, with contrasting hues melting together in lush shades of deep green, light hunter, and lime.

Bouncing from the molten and cooled, hardened clear sand—otherwise known as a windshield—the reflection of the brilliant morning light, with its rainbowed array of color, is poking my pupils with painless watery pleasure.

A flawlessly azure sky possesses my waking dreams with the dreams of millions of others, like secret treasures, hidden desires, even embarrassing lusts.

An unusual thunder begins to crescendo, shaking my immediate world like the passing of a thousand quadruple horse-drawn chariots. The bass tones intensify, reverberating within my chest, as a dark and glistening steel horse slowly invades my flank.

Mounted confidently on top of the loud and impressive steed sits a burly, kaleidoscopically tattooed bearded man. Somewhat stoic, and frightening, but in a strange way also peaceful, comfortable, and proud. Sitting tightly behind him, with her feet on pegs directly beneath the man's glutes, her knees bent high almost to his shoulders, and her arms tied around him like a backpack on a gradeschooler, hangs a slender, remarkably beautiful redhead. The wind causes her long, neat French braid to gently tickle the small of her back.

The spokes on the two-wheeled trophy spin invisibly, as if non-existent. I can't help but notice the redhead's lovely round posterior is just an inch above the exposed and rapidly rotating rear tire, dangerously close to the menacing rubber. She catches me not watching the road; she smiles, anyway. Yeah, she knows exactly what I was looking at.

Who are they? So free, so unencumbered by any restraints, traveling at speed, vulnerable, and yet, without a seeming care in the world. Hundreds of uncontrollable variables surround us all, and he appears to be in complete control of each unknown, her confidence in him displayed by her trust... and that smile. God, that smile.

Over the top of his dark sunglasses, he looks toward me with piercing eyes. I pretend not to notice. He nods, so I awkwardly nod back. With a sort of growl, the vibration and pounding thunder, unbelievably, increases, while the two who seem one on two wheels pull ahead. I want to accelerate and keep up—I want to go with them, leave everything behind—but I don't dare. I watch as they fade into the distance. I get the feeling that they are in love, kindred spirits, actually living their dreams—a dream that a flawlessly azure sky holds for hundreds of others. Certainly mine, in secret.

U-Turn

You've got three hundred miles behind you,
you've got a hundred more to go.
The glow stick-green dashboard
and orange needles
monitor your speed and fuel
as you push forward.

It's been a long day.
Your excitement to hit the road
made work drag on for centuries.
Your dry and tired eyes
roll in broken glass,
the side window open to a little of the cold.

Around you the vast emptiness
of the night embraces eternity.
Your son was sleeping beside you
in the dark;
now he's awake,
scanning the black quietness,

an alert owl on his perch.
You look at him
and back at the barren highway.
You feel how fortunate you are
to be with your eight-year-old,
both your faces wear an assuring grin.

You are happy but regret
all the time you've missed,

ball games and birthday parties.
He doesn't want to remember,
and you certainly can't forget.

He looks at you wide-eyed,
filled with admiration and love.
You smile and scruff his head.
He asks if this is like heaven.
You dry a tear and look above.

You decide right here, right now,
this is where you need to be.
It's time to change your ways.
No more extra nights and overtime days,
no clubhouses, bars, and whores to see.

You turn down a new road,
your radio tuned to a committed song.
With a smile, your owl hoots:
he needs to use the bathroom.
You're still a dad, you've been one all along.

RONALD BEY

Waking Up in a 6 x 9

Every morning I wake up to the sound of the food cart rolling into the unit, this being one of my reminders that another day has begun. I sit up, look at a picture of my family, then I pray for their safety and peace of mind. The air of the cell is dust-filled and has an odor no coat of paint can mask. Often, I get stuck staring at the dark square patch of wall in front of my desk speckled with toothpaste residue from years past. I brush my teeth in a sink that seems fit for a 1920s apartment; the drainage takes a lifetime, so usually I use the toilet so not to nasty the sink. No one wants to stare at your spent toothpaste. There's a window in the cell outlined in orange, the same as the door. I can't tell you why, but I have a nice view of a red brick wall—some architect's sick daily reminder that this is confinement. The only sound that pierces the stiff silence is the air vent's steady dust storm, which is ever-present. On a sunny day you can see the dust scurry through the air like snow in a slight breeze. The one word that can describe life in a cell is "decay"—slow death, the breakdown of a human psyche. But there is one highlight to my cell: books! Because even the most twisted fantasy is better than this reality that I share a 6 x 9 with a stranger, with a toilet built for a midget, a stone wall for a view, and whose floor stays riddled with dust no matter how much I sweep. Purgatory does exist. I know because I'm a resident.

Two Sides to a Coin

A lone body in a mass of sheets
Tossing and turning
Empty stomach growling and churning
Stale air blowing and souls burning.

A mistake from the past traps us in the here and now
It's two sides to a mind, what should I do, and how?
It's two sides to a coin, watch it go round and round.

Keys to the future are held in the past
Broken dreams, promises, and love that didn't last.
Peddled poison and sold lies just for petty cash
It's two sides to a coin, this flip may well be my last.

A flash of light, the dance of shadows
This brick house has fought many battles
It's two sides to a coin, when will it settle?
Could very well depend on the person you're sitting next to.

Thanksgiving

You wake up truly grateful for another day, a truly special day—Thanksgiving. You find humor in your happiness because not ten years ago you cursed the holiday, referring to it as "Indian Massacre Day," or the ever-classic "National Land Theft Day." Hmm. You have come a long way because today you know damn well the importance of this day, as well as all you have to be thankful for. As you close your eyes you give thanks to God for the miracle of life itself, a life that includes your two beautiful kids, your brother, your elders, your health and safety, your defeats, your victories, and your new but hard-to-maintain positive frame of mind. As you open your eyes, you look around your cell and take it all in, and the words of a wise minister come to mind: "You may have done what they said you did, but you are not who they say you are." This humbles you beyond measure. You realize that, even though confined, you've been spared such atrocities and violence that your ancestors, Jews, and victims of the Rwandan genocide suffered. Today you will enjoy the holiday meal without complaint because, even though it's not Mom's cooking, how many are born into starvation every hour? This Thanksgiving is no less special to you – now if only you can share your view without being called crazy.

If Only

If only you were born rich, life would be easy, right?
If only you weren't black, you could get a job, right?

If only you worked 9 to 5, you would be free, right?
If only you just sold weight, you wouldn't be in jail, right?

If only you weren't so disrespectful, but you so *hood*, right?
If only you could get out of your own way, you could change your
life, right?

If only you could earn respect through giving it, you would be a real
man, right?
If only you would treat her like one, she would be your queen, right?

If only you could get an education, you would effect change, right?
If only you didn't see a black president, race could be your excuse, right?

Now if only you think about what I said, maybe we can prove people
wrong, right?

LEE BREWER

Inevitable Conclusion

You will wake up at 9 a.m. tomorrow. The sun will shine on your bed from the open window. The sheets will feel soft, but the woman's skin next to you will feel softer. You will see shards of orange light on her naked back and impulsively trace these shapes along her spine. You will notice your hands—torn and beat—from years of ego and pride. How they inflicted so much pain and hate, but now only seek to protect and feel her next to you.

You will hear her murmur and roll over, stretching her arm and hair across your body. The smell and warmth of her will intoxicate your senses. You will think to yourself that nothing else matters, nothing can ever intrude upon these feelings of life and freedom. You will say to yourself that as long as she's here you can never feel sorrow, only solace and contentment, and when you begin to believe, the sun will begin to fade, and then you will know that she was never there. She was what you traded for the bottle of addiction in your fist. There will be no warmth, freedom, or life, only pain, hate, and sorrow.

Thanksgiving

It's Thanksgiving afternoon. Your mother stares at you through rogue hairs from across the table. She knows you're bombed. Your brother knows, your sister knows, the cat knows. But you don't care, because you're bombed. You feel thankful nobody has said anything to you about it. You feel thankful for the lager in the fridge and for the football game on television.

"Can you pass the potatoes?"

It's your sister. You look at her through frosty pupils. You think, *Get your own damn potatoes*, and then you pass the dish with a look of resentment. You feel the carbon from the lager building up in your gut. You belch. Everyone stares at you as if you'd just run over the dog.

"Well," you say. "That was good, Ma. I'm goin' in the other room to watch the game."

You stumble to the recliner. You feel thankful no one has said anything to you about being bombed. You feel thankful for the lager in your hand and for the football game on television. The cat jumps on your lap. It looks at you and meows. You love the cat. You lift it over your head and pretend it's the size of a lion. You pretend that you're keeping the great king of beasts at bay and ducking his spread claws.

"Hey!"

It's your mom.

"What the hell are you doin'?"

You can't say anything. You just start laughing at how absurd it must look. You're still holding the cat above your head. Your mother stares at you through rogue hairs. This makes it even funnier, and you continue to laugh. You put the cat back in your lap and feel thankful—thankful for lager, football, and lager.

ABDULLAH AS SIDDIQ

Still Life with the Ocean

As I sit back and relax,
I ponder the ocean.
Its many different changes
are people's emotions.
When the wind comes and blows,
it's easy to forget
that ocean was very calm,
but now it is morbid.
Happiness is when it's in a serene state,
but when those waves are thrashing,
that's when it's irate.
You can see it's sensitive,
just throw in a pebble.
That little reactionary movement shows frustration,
it's a little unsettled.
When it raises up like an arm, it's jumping for joy.
But when it's angry it leaves and comes back like a tsunami,
it's looking to destroy.
We are the ocean, we're here for a purpose.
Life isn't always easy, it's okay to be nervous.
Our body is made up mostly of the ocean.
I guess that's why it was so incumbent on me
to compare it to our emotions.

Untitled

Why is it that I'm made to feel like a stranger?
Being in this country it seems my life is always in danger
I don't want to lose my life
There's just so much racist anger

I'm not even carrying a knife
Please, upon my family bring no more strife
When you see me, don't be quick to kill
I have someone at home waiting, my wife

I'll make sure to stay still
You have to learn to relax and chill
I won't even sneeze
You're dealing with that old racist sickness, you're ill

You want me to freeze
With no hesitation I'll go to my knees
Me and my kids are taking their graduation pictures today, I just
want to say "Cheeze"
Me and my kids are taking their graduation pictures today, I just
want to say "Cheeze"

The Pen

The pen that was filled with ink
The pen that wrote that love letter
The pen with no top
The pen that stayed in my pocket
The pen whose ink spilled on my pants
The pen I lost in the back yard
The pen that I found
The pen that was my good luck charm
The pen that wrote "I'm sorry" one thousand times
The pen that left ink on my hands
The pen that I threw on the floor out of anger
The pen that was stolen
The pen that my teacher gave me
My brand new pen
The pen that drew the Mona Lisa
The pen that had just enough ink to write "I love you"
The pen that I kept upside down
My blue pen
The pen that everyone wanted
The pen I got stabbed with
The pen that wouldn't write
The pen that has only my fingerprints
The pen I left on the table
The pen that had water in it
The pen with the naked lady
The pen that had no ink
My pen

To Young Me

I'm so upset that you could not hear this when you were ten years old.
You had a very nasty disposition, and your attitude toward life you sold.
You really was hurting, just a scared little boy, turned toward selling
drugs because your mom couldn't afford a toy.
Just know that life will get better, there are a lot of twists and turns,
as long as there is a devil do your best not to trip over the curb.
His one job is to make you dumb.
Listen to what positive people say to you and to his deceit and tricks
you'll be numb.
Do not have those drugs, it's better to be sober, with a clear mind going
through life that thing between your ears will be like a four-leaf clover.
The people that you're hanging with really don't care anything about
you; if they did they'd push you toward greatness, and with your
potential they'd never doubt you.
Do not drop out of school because education is a good luck charm,
if you quit you'll only be setting yourself up for self-harm.
Hanging in the streets and being with those older guys may seem cool
until you're locked up for life and realize you were one of devil's tools.
Do not allow violence, girls, money, and that false reality be your focus.
After being on this planet for thirty years you'll realize that that life
was nothing but hocus pocus.
The most important people in your life are your family.
That fake "love" your boys will say they have for you is nothing but
a scam.
Trust me, they want to be around you because of that good quality
you have of being loyal, letting them use you until you're in prison
of six-feet deep in the soil.
Do not allow anger to consume you, and with this letter trust in
me, my advice I'm trying to relay is to do the right thing, and focus
is the key.

REAL RELL

Honor Thy Life

Honor thy creator, thy fertile land, thy seed planter, thy roots of a small plant that blossom into a beautiful flower, thy showers that help thy flowers develop, thy growth of a garden, from one region to another, thy sunrise allowing thy sun's rays to shine in thy mist of any weather, thy warm wind that blows to dry thy rich soil, thy kingdom, thy home of thy gracious animals, thy oxygen in thy air breathed by all mankind, thy embryo, evolving to a fetus, to a toddler, thy nurtured young child, maturing into an adult, honoring thy life, thy mother and thy father.

Thy end!

I Love July

I love July, and the reason why is because, on the second of July, 1992, I was born. Plus, it's the summertime, and two days later is the Fourth, where there's fireworks, music in the sky from live concerts, water fights and cookouts, ice cold beverages being poured, my auntie enjoying her special medicine for her glaucoma, the prettiest women wearing the skimpiest linen that make my uncle say, "I don't need to bring contacts to the beach to see all this booty and beauty." Besides vacation, we take trips to the amusement parks—Lake Compounce, Six Flags, Disney World, Universal Studios—and take pictures for the extended family at the reunion, where we laugh, sing, dance . . . Boy, do I love July! And when next year come, we do it all again.

Dedicated to Tamika Owens, the Love of My Life

MARQUIS JACKSON

Self-portrait, 2010

Long black-colored corn-braided hair
Hanging out the back of a black doo-rag cap.

Caramel-colored skin, high-structured cheekbones
Camouflage-fatigue skin, thick like Nestle Quick
Wrinkle-free and compressed tightly
With a couple of slash marks here and there
From the years of battle tears.

Light brown cloudy filtered eyes
Hazy from the years of passersby
Those days of passersby
By-by until another time.

Button-less shirt with butterfly collar
A pair of brown zipper-less slip-on pants
Black on black feet protectors, size 9.

Two back pockets filled with lint and emptiness
And with the hope of one day obtaining
And gaining the papers of a parolee-inductee.

Letter to Myself as a Young Man

Dear Macho,

Today you will play the basketball game of your life—literally. You will play this game at Quinnipiac University in front of a crowd of fifteen thousand cheering and jeering fans. But don't mind them—you will have a good game, not a great game but a good game, nevertheless. You will score 27 points and have 9 assists. But as the game comes down to the wire you will become arrogant and forget the art and technique of proper free-throw shooting. You will forget to heed the instructions you received from Jim Calhoun three years prior, when you attended the UConn Summer League Basketball Camp, which set your parents back a couple hundred bucks for the week-long extravaganza.

But I digress.

You will be fouled and put on the line with three seconds left in regulation, with your team down by one point. Stay focused and remember the mechanics: EYES ON BASKET, ELBOWS IN, BEND YOUR KNEES, AIM JUST ABOVE THE FRONT END OF THE RIM, AND FOLLOW THROUGH...SWISH. You've done this hundreds of times. If only you knew that victory has 100 fathers, but defeat is left orphaned. Keep in mind that when all is said and done these two free throws will mean more to you than just two points. Because if you miss, they will lead you to make two rash decisions. First, you will quit the once-prized varsity basketball team. Then, you will decide to quit school. Which will lead you down a path of SELF-DESTRUCTION.

So, in conclusion, this is your One Shining Moment in Time. Please don't squander away this golden opportunity to make something out of your life. Remember, take your time while shooting these free throws. As I said earlier, they represent more than just two points. They also represent two pivotal choices in life you will inevitably have to make. Through this situation I've learned that the ultimate measure of a man is not where he stands in the moments of comfort and convenience, but where he stands at times of challenge and controversy. So, stay focused and sink these two free throws for us and change the course of my life—I mean *our* life.

P.S. I am writing to you from a state maximum-security prison, for the two free throws I failed to see the significance of.

So much depends upon

what is considered
true

glazed with blatant
fallacy

hidden behind barrier
blocks

This is just to say

I have beaten
the odds
that were stacked
in abundance

and which
you were probably
hoping
would break me

forgive me
it was easy
it all
depends on within

The Bike

The shiny chrome Dino GT bike on the store's rack.
The bike I must have.
The bike I have no money for.
The bike I rode right out the store.
The bike with the chrome frame.
The bike that drove all my friends insane.
The bike with the front pegs.
The bike with the back pegs.
The bike with the pegs that really went to my head.
The bike that cruised through the 'hood.
The bike that was always up to no good.
The bike with the front brakes.
The bike with the back brakes.
The bike that needs brakes.
The bike with the rusted chain.
The bike I accidentally left out in the rain.
The bike that caught a flat.
The bike that got patched up—ASAP.
The bike I parked out back.
The bike I stole.
The bike that got stolen from *me*.
The bike I cried for.
The bike I got to ride no more.
The bike I drove.
The bike that drove *me*.
The bike I must get back.
The bike with the unlimited gears: fast and faster.
The bike with the chrome spokes.
The bike with the black leather seat.
The bike I used to stop with my feet.

The bike I loved.
The bike I thought loved me.
The bike I lost.
The bike of my dreams.
Now the bike of my nightmares.
The bike...
The bike...
   What bike?
My bike, the chrome Dino GT.
   You mean *his* chrome Dino GT?

Thunderica

Here she comes with her cousins, Lightning and Fury.
She cracks the midnight skies like a hairline crack
In a panoramic view to the universe.
With total abandon and disregard for humans' creations
She works her magic and justifies her reason for existence.
Her best friend, Loud Rumbling, who accompanies her to the ball,
Is earth-shattering and intimidating.
The moment is tense, as if something epic is about to occur.
We await her punchline with trepidation.
Can you hear her?
Can you feel her?
(Her screams and quakes are like our yearning to be,
And exist,
In a world of uncertainty.)
After a short pause in the mayhem,
She dissipates,
As if she had never existed.
The only evidence left in her wake is
Split trees,
And dashed dreams
Of an ordinary, uneventful day.

Where I'm From

I'm from a place that's been strategically built near highways and
byways for easy exits –
I'm from tenement housing, with broken windows and urine-stained
hallways –
From where grandmothers are thirty-five with a baby on the way –
Where rap music blares from every car through weed smoke-tinted
windows –
Where there are big dreams of making it out, with no road map to
get there –
I'm from where probable cause is established by the color of your
skin, and stop and frisk is standard operating procedure –
A place where the young are killed in a crude sport of stand-your-ground –
Where any Negro will suffice to solve a crime before reelection day –
I'm from a place that is never sunny but always seems to be hot –
A place that all ye who enter here, abandon all hope –
I'm from the land of pipe dreams and crack fiends –
Where if you speak proper English or pursue higher education, you're
trying to be white –
Where you get more respect for serving a prison sentence than return-
ing from college with a master's degree –
I'm from a place where you are taught vices at an early age –
A place where there is a liquor store on every other corner –
A place that prefers to cast bullets over ballots –
A place where every crime carries a maximum and a minimum –
Where cancer sticks are marketed to the youth, to look cool –
Where material possessions equate to an individual's worth –
I'm from where the end justifies the means –
I'm from where *The Cosby Show* is a fictional depiction of family life –
A place where poverty runs rampant –
A place where it's profit over principles –

I'm from where the people never achieved the American Dream, but experienced the American Nightmare –

A place where they profit from slave labor, then imprison the slave –

A place with a depressed economy, based on a depressed education system being the salvation for a depressed people –

A place where the dominant culture feels you add no value –

Where you live for the moment, because tomorrow ain't promised –

Where the life expectancy is twenty-five –

A place where you duck strays from frustrated youths stuck in their ways –

A place where the come-up is your main priority, and if you impede that progress you can potentially become a victim –

A place where the churches are the shadiest and the congregations begin praying to God for so long that they are now atheists.

A place where the majority of the occupants are criminal-minded –

Where the victim steadily becomes the victimizer –

Where the conventional way of earning a living is perceived as senseless, unproductive, and unappealing –

I'm from a place where they don't accept second-class non-violently –

A place where welfare is handed down from generation to generation –

Where Section 8 tells the mother of your child you can't sleep over –

A place that reeks of despair and hopelessness –

I'm from a place where one out of three of the males are in jail or on their way –

A place where a two-parent home is a rarity –

A place where a positive male role model is an endangered species –

Where cousins and siblings grow up in the same apartment –

A place where on the first of the month every bank is jam-packed –

A place where employment is denied because of previous legal infractions –

I'm from a place where we never received our 40 acres and a mule –

Do you recognize the place I call home? If you squint, you might miss it. But if you open your eyes wide you would see that it is the land of the free and home of the brave.

Do you enjoy the view?

Premature

Lately, my pen has run out of ink.
You try explaining the unexplainable.
     Why me?
Each time I pick up the pen my fingers break from heartache.
Somehow I've become accustomed to this feeling of *What if?*
     Is this my fault?
This can't be what life has to offer me.
And now, each night, as I rot on my cot, I count calendars. Five, six, maybe seven. They represent the bane of my anguish.
And each night I come up with the same number: Life. And when I become mentally fatigued, I spell it out.
Unlucky me.
Nobody visits anymore.
It's true: joy is easier to share than pain.
And then, last night it happened.
The doctor came into my wife's hospital room and said, "Your daughter will make it."

Unfulfilled

I would rather be great than lame, living life on my own terms.

I would rather deal in absolutes—black and white, truth and facts—than to deal in uncertainties, "What if's?"

I would rather be extreme in my defense of liberty than moderate in my pursuit of justice.

I would rather matter than to sit idly by on the sideline of life, watching it pass me by.

I would rather be visible than invisible.

I would rather speak truth to power than to cower in a corner on my knees.

To be clear, truth is better than fiction, sobriety better than addiction, virtue better than vice.

I would rather be woke than broke, living life on a tightrope with little hope.

I would rather have hope in a hopeless place.

I would rather be an optimist than a pessimist, because I would rather live.

I would rather see the world from above than below.

When they go low, I am high. This is the way I choose to get by. Please let me by.

I would rather be a consequence of my own making than inconsequential in your eyes.

The lie we tell ourselves.

Unfortunately, life is designed to be understood backwards, but lived forwards.

I would rather hear the truth than to hear unjust words to justify a convenient lie.

What a lie.

I would rather make the impossible seem possible than to roll over and die without trying.

I would rather eat beans and have my freedom than be served cake and be a slave.

Shall I cut off my nose to spite my face, and not face my fate courageously, or shall I auction off my future to thrive now, in this present state?

I would rather choose to do neither.

JUAN BOTELLO

A View of Myself

Gray sweats with a white T
Fresh white high-tops
Brown stone skin
With darker brown eyes
Nose of a fighter
With lips for a dame
Silky short hair
Connected to a head filled with comprehension
A chest that holds a loyal heart
I am merely a young man, but a man nonetheless
Dressed in flesh and blood fatigues
Some say a soldier
Intellectual thoughts
With a stoner's persona
On a humble path of life
With ambition to strive
And devoted to overcoming obstacles
I am on a journey...
...to one day be in Jannah*.

* "Jannah" is the Islamic word for "paradise."

NORMAN GAINES

Self-Portrait

Strip me of my cover, my skin
See I for what I am
Look to discover and you will find
One mind, one body, one soul
Colorless as the transparent sky
Defined by the speech of my words
And intent of my actions
I'm an individual
Bounded not by group or race
Others declare...
To proclaim me black
Denies the brown for which you see
The brown of my skin, my hair, my eyes
Inherited from the various shades of continents
The water, the air, their beginnings, their ends.

Strip me of my cover, my skin
Look to discover and you will find
A noun amongst a menagerie of nouns
A person of a zoo of people
Mirrored by the hands of humanity
Singled out by his emphatically unique prints.

Strip me of my cover, my skin
See I for what I am
Look to discover and you will find
A self-portrait of you!

Poseidon's Will

Did Poseidon intend to embrace Asia when he tore through her villages and shops?

Did he mean to secure her treasures when he washed it all into the sea?

And did he not know her prisms would fall to squares when the mountain crumbled over Zeus's shadow?

And why did he stop at Obama's shores?

Was he greeting Man with "Namasté," or warning that his parting was near?

I guess time one day will give reason,
for when the boss acts, none can question.

Fundamental laws forbid queries to be asked of hallowed suggestions, and as servants in life all must remain true.

From the moment the unborn children came to be, understanding was made wise.

"Be not consumed by limited visions and you shall be freed from your betraying hearts."

Yet Man complains of the cloud's flooding rain when the roots of his air suffer pangs extreme.

And the women—
Look at how they labor alone for choosing to rear babies
By beasts unworthy.

And who doth not wonder
About the child born to fulfill thy mother's love
Addiction
When it's birthed with strong needs that'll remain unattended?

Is there no extent to a person's blinding desire?

Again, I guess only the future will tell.

Until then, pray Poseidon allows us the freedom to rejoice on the sands of Cape Cod and bring not down its neighbor's symbol of liberty.

For Man is truly lost when he's robbed of thy land's comfort and safety of freedom.

Let us pray his patience wears thin not on our young and alloweth them the chance to right thy parents' wrongs.
And let us pray the youth is granted the phenomenon of age and be not ended before the growth of their molars.

Poseidon, allow your mercy to give us the leave of minutes
So we can bring death to our vain tries.

You have our word—if thy speech turns to lies the hearts of thy family's body you may pry.
And outdo our internecine pride,
This time not with a tear
But with one last cry.

As so written!

I Miss Prison

Jamaal is an ex-con who has been home for 5 years, 3 months and 2 days after serving 12 long years in prison for manslaughter. He started serving his sentence, his first and only offense, at 17, and was released at age 29, a few days before his 30th birthday. He's accomplished a lot since he was set free, but it hasn't been easy.

When he came home, he had nowhere to go. His mother and grandmother had both died while he was in prison, the mother of a drug overdose at age 41, the grandmother of a combination of diabetes, high blood pressure, and old age. She was 72, God bless her. Jamaal never knew his father's side of the family. His younger sister, Keisha, had moved down south and started a new life with the rest of the family a couple of years before Jamaal was released. And all his friends were either dead, in prison, or still in the street life—the life that had robbed him of his teens and all of his twenties. He certainly wasn't going to lose his thirties.

So, long story short, with nowhere else to go, he went to a shelter, got on welfare, and entered whatever programs New York City had to offer recently released prisoners. The program helped him find shelter and work. He applied for school and did his first two years through online correspondence courses. Now, with a steady job as a restaurant manager, a wife, a kid, and the proud owner of a $250,000 home, he finds himself entertaining a collect call from a man he had looked up to as a father while in prison, a man named Ahmad, an African American Muslim serving life for a double homicide.

Jamaal had promised Ahmad he would never forget him—he would never forget the man who taught him to read, to value education and value life, among other things, and he kept true to his promise. Once a month he sends a few dollars and photos and allows him to call the house.

So, after a few minutes of exchanging hello's and how-you-doing's, Ahmad asks, "How do you do it? You know—manage to stay home and keep succeeding where others fail."

And Jamaal replies, "I miss prison."

"You miss prison?"

"Yeah, man, I miss prison. I miss the way the cell door opened periodically, signaling me when to wake up, when to go to rec, and when to shower.

"I miss the way the COs told me I was done eating, done recreating, done bathing, and done being awake.

"I miss the way the cards and dominoes slammed down on the tables, and the sounds of laughter from the mouths of those who wasted time while doing it.

"I miss writing people who never wrote back.

"I miss waiting for the money orders that were never sent.

"I miss being in the cell and smelling the air that exited another man's ass.

"I miss hearing the code blues, oranges, and purples.

"I miss sleeping and dreaming of being home and then waking up inside the cell.

"I miss seg. I miss the no-contact contact visits, and most of all I miss being forced to strip naked in front of another man and being called derogatory names by the rookie cop that became captain."

"And why do you miss all that, son?" Ahmad asks.

"Because all that reminds me of my favorite line," Jamaal says. "The words I miss most when things get hard out here."

"And what's that, Jamaal?"

"I miss saying, 'If I go home, I swear to God I'm not coming back!'"

"I hear that, son," Ahmad says. "I hear that." And with that the phone clicks and terminates the call.

And, right on cue, Jamaal's wife walks in as he places the phone on the table. "Who was that, baby?"

"Ahmad," Jamaal replies.

"So, what did he have to say?"

"The same as always. He said hello."

Then his wife starts up by saying, "Babe, you know every time he calls, I hear you guys talking, and every time I ask what you guys talked about you say, 'Nothing, he just said hello.'"

Then Jamaal counters, "You're damn right about that, and until you get on the phone that always allows you to say 'Hello' and always hangs up before you can say 'Goodbye,' all you need to know is that he said 'Hello'—for one day that Hello will mean Goodbye."

And, as any great woman would, she decoded her husband's words, looked deep into his eyes, and said, "I don't know what it's like to be in prison, so I can't remind you of the pain that keeps you from going in, but I can remind you of the love that'll keep you from going back!"

J.V. HARVEY

Taped to My Wall: Sunrays

Just above my head is a mirage of constant reminders of why I would never like to see these walls again, starting with my daughter. I was incarcerated when she was just two, just a few months from turning three. In the first picture, from left to right, I'm holding her; she's a baby. The time chronicle of her growth plays out like a projection of a young life I have never seen, and I can't go back and replay that part of the movie.

But certain pictures I have the glory to stretch across my memory. I was there. In that picture she fell asleep eating goldfish crackers in her highchair. That one the nurse took, when we first met, St. Francis Hospital, 7:45 PM, April 16, 1998. Everyone was worried because she hardly cried. "Yes, I have arrived now, baby need sleep." In that picture she was just learning how to walk, and shortly after that a decision I made walked me in a different direction!

In certain pictures of her you can pick out my features—my nose, my lips—beautifully scary, it's me in a sundress. Then over time on my wall you can see her mother's face creeping in. Ironic, the same eyes I fell in love with.

That's the sunshine on my wall.

The saddest part taped to these cinderblocks is three obituaries. My aunt died young of throat cancer. She stopped sending me to the store for cigarettes because I would return with lies and candy. "How in hell they run out of cigarettes, they always carry Lucys, boy." Then my uncle—his fast, dope-filled life finally slowed him down. He died in jail, so at times I feel bad having him taped to these walls. And last is a best friend. We'd known each other since the age of ten. He's alive in certain spots on the wall. He brings some excitement with his motorcycles, flashes of memories when we rode together, challenging one another to switch to faster gears, the peace of happiness, speed, and freedom. I always wore a helmet, but he said it was a distraction, it made him hot. I wish he knew how they've been upgraded.

But he brings a special piece of sun to my room: his daughter. That's her and my daughter at Great Adventure two years ago. That's them on the first day of school together this year. That's them during a sleepover. Oh, that one, that's them at a birthday party. That's them repeating friendship.

Brightening up my walls! SUNRAYS!

JOSÉ LUIS PESANTE, JR.

One Smooth Cat

Uncle J.R. is quite the character. His trademark goatee-style mustache and beard are as much a part of him as the cans of Budweiser surgically glued into the palms of both hands.

Whenever I think of my Uncle J.R., I can't help but reminisce of Chinese kung-fu slippers, Stetson cologne, E-Z Wider tobacco rolling paper, and a popular song by George Michael that still haunts me: *Shoulda known better than to be your friend, a wasted chance that I been given . . .*

Those were the best of days, driving around with my uncle jamming to the music of the times and hitting on every woman we came upon. J.R. had a pair of bionic green eyes that cut right through anyone he gazed at. Short and pot-bellied, he labeled himself "husky." Sometimes he wore his hair in a kind of Puerto Rican version of a mullet. It flowed back sort of like a Dee-ay and turned into a long tail of hair that reached the middle of his shoulders. My brothers and I tried to mimic Uncle J.R.'s hairdo but could never get it like his.

Every morning, whether rain, snow, hail, or sleet, J.R. was working on someone's car. He was the neighborhood Meineke Man. If your brakes squealed, someone would usually joke, "Uh-oh! Better get to J.R." Because of this, my uncle always smelled like high octane fuel, made worse by the liter of Stetson cologne he tried to mask his choice of career with. He almost always wore a tee shirt decorated with oil stains, but they usually matched his blackened hands and fingernails. I remember thinking his olive-colored skin looked extra tan in the summer, but his complexion would only darken with the season changes because of the increase in work he would get.

My uncle is a very proud Puerto Rican. His orange Chevy Nova was dressed in so many flags representing Puerto Rico that it looked as if every day was a celebration of the tiny Caribbean island. When-ever we drove around in his car, it was so much fun. He would burn rubber at every red light and honk his fancy horn that sounded the melody of *La cucaracha! La cucaracha!* On the dashboard were black and white stickers of rabbits with the word PLAYBOY written in capital letters along the borders. J.R. was one smooth cat.

He taught me how to help his "special" plants grow by pissing into his magic garden and watering it with any backwash left over inside his tall cans of beer. My first memories of Bruce Lee include us sitting around Uncle J.R.'s VCR-TV and later practicing the moves at the end of the movie. It always amazed me how he could show us how to punch, block, and roundhouse kick without spilling one drop of Budweiser. We also learned how to make a girl blush with a few choice words. J.R. always knew exactly what to say to the ladies.

Last time I saw my uncle, he looked just as I remembered. The lines in the palms of his hands were caked up with grit, grease, and motor stains. He wore a single earring of a mini-PLAYBOY in his left ear and smelled like a cowboy. Some young cutie, fifteen years younger than him, sat on his lap twirling his long hair between her fingers while I admired my uncle. I wondered if he still had it in him, so, just for kicks, I tried an old karate punch. Before I could hit him, he crushed my fist by blocking the punch with a good ol' can of beer. That's my Uncle J.R. for ya . . . One smooth cat.

Ode to My Ghetto

Born into my world on a July afternoon in 1974
My ghetto cradled me to its bosom.
I can still remember Her beating heart—
The way She stared at my nakedness
Through the hospital windows.
There are many a Ghetto across the land—
But none like mine.
Dressed in shards of broken bottles and spent beer cans,
She glitters!
Her walk whispers softly like thunder between alleyways.
Her sweet scent of urine
Bounces off the walls of abandoned buildings.
There are many a Ghetto across the land—
But none like mine.
Her soothing voice sings like punctured speakers
When police sirens ring.
Empty marijuana bags snag
In the cracked pavement of Her gapped teeth.
I love Her—
But She always finds a way
To make me love Her more...
This Ghetto of mine is like fine wine.
Like a wet dream multiplied.
Like a shootout in a movie.
Like candy-coated raindrops.
Late-night, alcohol-fueled arguments spill from Her lips,
Warmly melting into my ears.
Early morning, dogs bark at gunshots,
Warmly melting into my ears.
She is so supportive—

The way heroin addicts
Lean against Her light poles to nod off.
The way STDs
Ooze like honey from Her nostrils.
The way She exhales,
Her smog fills my lungs with asthma—
It's breathtaking!
The way Death kneels
At Her feet to pray—
It's heavenly!
I can still hear Her beating heart—
Especially when She stares at me
Through the prison windows . . .
She misses me.
There are many a Ghetto across the land—
But none like mine.

A Blink in Time

A ways to go before I learn
Life turns and flips and flips and turns
The days fly by, no time for thought
A pause for breath, a breath to burn

Each night I sleep is one more bought
Until the morn' who can't be caught
A week, a month, a year, a blink
The days fly by, no time to think

Gray hairs appear, gray thoughts I think
The kids are grown, my folks are pink
So sore from chores, my body pains
My cup of yore I wish to drink

Before I die I pray to claim
From birth to death a man became
A blink in time, a simple stain
A blink in time, a simple stain.

Lead Rain

So much depends
upon
my assassin's poor
aim
showering me with
glazed bullets
puncturing my limbs
with lead rain

This is just to say

I have swallowed
death once, twice
I've regurgitated it.
Thrice I've risen, only
to be knocked down again.
Forgive me, today has
not been a good day.

There You Are

Where is the heart's home?
    Is it where memories are glazed
    like nectar-filled passion fruit?
    Or embedded into your footprints
    like an Indian rain dance?
    Is it inside your giggles
    like tickles?
    Or deep within
    like déjà vu times two?
    Maybe it's in la-la land
    where thoughts birth emotions
    like magic spells and love potions.
    Or is it all inside your head?

Sitting on the Lips of Morning

Awaking to the persistent buzzing of my alarm clock is what I miss most. And most of all I miss the silence of my bedroom after insisting the persisting buzzing gradually fade away.

What I miss most is dreaming of a dream where I'm lying on my soft pillow-top bed. And most of all I miss sitting on the lips of morning, yawning at the new day while tickling my toes in the fuzz of my slippers.

What I miss most is the scent of fried eggs igniting the air with flames of sizzling yolk. And most of all I miss walking into the kitchen to find my wife's every lovely curve standing in front of the stove, sculpting breakfast sandwiches out of bricks of Italian bread.

What I miss most is the squeaking staircase singing to the tune of my children's feet. And most of all I miss watching them stumble to the dinner table, still half asleep, to taste the masterpiece so deliciously known as family time.

NATHANIEL BOYKIN

The Ghost of Irony

A Ghost of Irony came into my block unit, flying around spreading great joy to each and every one. He looked very scary and evil, but he was good and kind. The ghost looked like a little goblin. He was four feet tall with a head bigger than his body. He had green and black eyes that would scare the pants off you. He would grin at you with raggedy, rotten, jagged teeth and nasty, pukey-smelling breath that would make you nauseous. He surprised everyone with extraordinary gifts. He would give you seven days of freedom, three days of trailer visits with any woman and hotel room service. Finally, after each wish was granted, officers would check us back in the jail wearing long white robes with hummingbirds flying around them.

The Ghost of Irony was the best thing that ever happened in our prison.

There's an Eagle in My Heart

There's an eagle in my heart that wants to get out.

When I was a child, I allowed my eagle to get out by riding my bike out of my familiar neighborhood to explore new horizons and nice scenery. While I was riding, I would briefly stare into the blue sky and watch the songbirds flying. Mother Nature is so beautiful. I would listen to the whistling winds and feel the cool breeze and the sunny sensation in my face. My friend and I would ride past this vicious black and white German Shepherd barking from behind his fence. We also saw a tan cat watching the dog while hanging off tree branches.

As I see all this, there's an eagle in my heart that wants to get out, so I keep riding faster and faster. I pass by lots of black, white, and Latino people walking on the street. It's a multicultural parade of people.

I continue to ride my bike across town, from the north end to the east side of Bridgeport. My grandfather works for G.E., which is on the east side. My friends and I came here to see his four-door blue Cadillac Brougham sedan with a white ragtop. I was only 13 years old, and my friends and I were so proud of my granddad.

There's an eagle in my heart that wants to get out and be just like my granddad.

This is Just to Say

I will be going to the North End Boys Club after school
to play basketball and other activities that they have.
I will be home at 7 PM.
Please cover up my supper and
put it away in the oven until I get home.
Don't forget to run my bathwater
and make sure it's not too hot.

THE DOVES

My First House

The first house I lived in was small because it was actually an apartment. The run-down two-bedroom apartment that was missing the other bedrooms for the roaches and rats that invaded my residence like the U.S. invaded Iraq. It had the leaky ceiling and a paint job a painter would feel disrespected for. The bucket in the middle of the floor caught the water leaking from the ceiling. The cadence of the drops was symbolic of the second hand on the ancient clock hugging the wall. The renegade roaches were like visiting family members that didn't want to leave. They also claimed everything from the cereal to the bathroom, as well as all my toys. The squeaky wooden floors with the many splinters had me picking pieces of wood out of my feet daily. I always wondered what happened to the back yard and the white picket fence. But I was constantly reminded this was not TV and the Projects don't come with those things. The ugly two-seater couch was my favorite place to have a royal rumble with all my wrestlers. The apartment was so small, it was like comparing an ant to an elephant. The smell of flavored wood was constant as my mother burned incense around the apartment. I remember when I put a penny in the socket, the feeling was electrifying.

CHRISTOPHER T. BERCHEM

Four Haiku

Light fades, summer ends
Dark creeps across the prison
Shadows of darkness

Summer heat grows cool
Gardens yield fragrant produce
Winds blow to test trees

Children walk cold streets
Demanding their candy treats
But not anymore

Autumn in my heart
Once our love burned hot and bright
Fading into night

Structured Search for Meaning

So much depends upon finding meaning.
Poetry is full of symbolism
From which a man can take his own gleaning,
Whether positive or criticisms.

Statistics are sometimes called worse than lies,
But when done correctly will uncover
Truth, if your sample is a good size,
And hidden truth you often discover.

Chemistry relies on so many things,
The types of atoms and how they connect,
Their shape, and electrons each atom brings,
But what it says is never quite direct.

Many don't see beauty in little things,
But there is joy as known only by kings.

This is just to say

I owe you more
than you think
Maybe you know
I'd be dead
if you were not
there for me
but you also saved my soul.

Untitled

Go home and write?
Where, where, where is home? Is my home a cell? A tiny, shared room?
Eight different cells in eight months.

They say, "Home is where the heart is."

Who do I love?
I have no children. My lover is a heroin addict in a rehab center for
women. That is not my home. I still love my brothers and my mom, but
I've left my childhood home, and my home is not with my brothers.

What do I love?
I love numbers: natural, rational, irrational, imaginary.
Can I make a home in a non-Euclidean or Minkowski space?
I love chemistry and physics; thermodynamics, kinetics, quantum
mechanics and quantum electro-dynamics.
Can I find a home adrift, in a Sea of Dirac?
I love philosophy: Socrates, Bacon, Hume, and Kafka.
Can I live in Plato's world of ideal forms? Does home exist? Do *I* exist?
I love religion: Buddha, Krishna. I've chosen Catholic.
Maybe in time I will choose to make a monastery home?
How does one become a monk? Can a monk have a lover?
Can a monk have a record?

What makes a house a home?
She likes carpets, fluffy pillows, curtains, and warm colors. I like a
few bright lights, glass tables, and mirrored walls—lenses to focus
and bend light, prisms to refract it.

My mom crossed the Atlantic to find her home, and my brother's
home takes him across the Pacific.

I'm sorry.
I'll take an F.
My work is incomplete.
I can write,
but I can't go home.

To Charles Lutwidge Dodgson

Since I was a boy I have been a fan.
Your works were fun, but now that I am a man
They've become a source of inspiration,
A creative sort of invitation
        To see reality in a different way.
        Your stories seem to be riddled with nonsense,
        With silly grammar and lots of word play.
           Neither time nor space seem to be constant.
One plus one does not always equal two;
Such is the case in vector mathematics.
The most solid things are lots of nothing.
Being absurd is not being untrue.
Brains are often left on automatic
Because extra work we are loathing.
        Math uncovers hidden information
           Which can lead us to a revelation,
        But it takes creative application
        Interpreting quantification.
Mathematics was your primary career,
But photography and games you held dear.
People know you best by your writer's hand,
Alice's Adventures in Wonderland.

MARTIN P. GINGRAS

Ode to My Pillow

Lo, comfort hangs
Like a bat in a cave.
These walls of cement close around me
Neither mattress nor hands can comfort.
Blanket means head support of warmth.

Hark, I see the object!
Looking upon that pillow
Rolling atop that cart
Like a conquering king atop his escort
Pushed along solemnly like the Ark of the Covenant.

It arrives.

I take the pillow like it holds all my dreams
As if to dishevel it is to ruin its purpose.
The feel of plastic wrapped around fire-retardant material
Like an ordinary chalice sitting on a table.

I open this pillow swiftly
Placing the case around it.
I place it gently on the bed
Like a child fast asleep.
I lie down, my head engulfed in pillow
Like lying in a field of grass and moss.
I close my eyes
My body resting like a bear in winter.
Comfort comes to my neck and shoulders

A forgotten comfort, like some nameless memory.

Lo, five months of hell, lifting to heaven
My mind fades into this pillow
Like a sun into a cloud
Like a fish in water, light fading to dark
Worries melt from me
Like ice in the first blossom of spring.

The moral:
Large things can come and go
But . . .
Small things overseen should be held
Like fleeting drops of dew in your hands.

Justice Curse

Prison walls, though they are absurd
Caging a heart like a songbird
Bringing me down to surrender
My soul stagnates like that of curd

Walls forcing mind to meander
Leaving me less than ever tender
I sleep my life like a cold bear
Life stopped in a traffic bender

Each ripping a larger tear
Dreams of freedom caught in a snare
Trying to read, always to doze
Few seem to see, never to care

Seeing one's self from head to toes
Permanently body in death throes
Eyes, mind, soul never yet to close
Eyes, mind, soul never yet to close

CHARLES LOGAN

Untitled

74 Cabot Street. Turquoise blue, two rooms, three brothers—you do the math. Two at the foot, one at the head. My house smells of baking soda and lead. Mommy says my big brother's bad!

I feel him, though, like the dad I never had, and his red and black Pumas are effectively tuff. Posters on the wall: Erik B. and Rakim, NWA, which had its new sound, but Mommy wasn't hearing it. "Boy, turn that #@%! down! And clean this room."

Clothes on the floor, bed unmade. There's my book: *Birds Fly, Bears Don't*. I'm hungry now. Our kitchen offers cereal and dry milk, a gas stove, a refrigerator hum, phone on the wall (but it's not on). I take my bowl to the favorite part of my house, the living room sofa, but Mommy doesn't let us sit on the couch. That's all right, the carpet's soft and the TV's on my favorite show: "Awww, what's up, doc?"

MOUNT YETI

I Need a Cardiac Massage

Where, oh where, is Michael Jackson?
The King of Kings,
The god of gods,
Is he walking on the moon
Or rehearsing in another dimension?
He had made time irrelevant.
When he sang
The universe exploded,
When he danced
The earth shuddered
As if being stricken by an asteroid.
Being a star must cause insomnia,
He needed sleeping pills for sedation,
For Michael loved the world so much
He trimmed his nose
And bleached his skin.
When will he return?
Thus, Justin Bieber can stop
"Never Say Never."

Destiny

What is law?

Please wait, darling!
This is not like food
You have to eat immediately
Because you're hungry.

Please wait, darling!
This is not like speed
You have to push instantly
Because you're craving.

Please wait, darling!
This is not like sex
You have to taste blindly
Because you're at puberty.

Please wait, darling!
This is not like larceny
You have to break in
Because there is an urge.

Please wait, darling!
This is not like war
You have to charge
Because there is an enemy.

I'm innocent until proved otherwise
You do not have to be in a hurry to tell me:
I'm a minority

I'm from the inner city
I've never seen my father
My mother lives in poverty.

I'm innocent until proved otherwise
You do not have to be in a hurry to tell me:
I'm lazy
I'm ugly
I talk too much
I need to change.

I'm innocent until proved otherwise
You do not have to be in a hurry to tell me:
I do not have a private attorney
The ACLU will not help me
I do not have anything
My family has abandoned me.

I'm innocent until proved otherwise
You do not have to be in a hurry to tell me:
You can invade my body
You can take my property
You can rape my sanity
You can molest my liberty.

Or:
What is crime?

Be Man

The people I love the best
are from rank and file.
They get up to work and go to bed for rest,
humble, like shrubs in the forest
they are cushions for the falling tree.
Fathers, mothers, brothers, sisters, sons, and daughters—
surely you know Good Samaritans, Quakers and Schindler,
but please remember your neighbors,
pastors, Mike, Brenda, Mr. Aldrich, and a nurse called Marianne.
They're candles in the cold, dark night,
burning themselves to make you shine.

I love people who stand straight, like a poplar.
Bitter wind and blazing sun cannot blind their eyes.
If keeping faith means to walk an extra mile
they'll embrace desert storms like a lonely star.

I want to be with people who rejoice when you win,
greet you when you're lost,
and do not give up on you when you're the last.
They are from the heavens and not rare on earth
—with them, I'll be brave to jump from the sky,
but scared to make them cry.

The world of the human is not a perfect one.
Life has never been easy, and death hardly a surprise.
A gesture of kindness or a hint of reassurance
can carry a person far and wide.

KYLLE BREWER

Bingo

In the summer of 2001
I don't know what it was
Mind elevation
Or a super buzz

My brain was working
Like a supercomputer
Processing and retaining this data
Now I'm thinking kind of like a Buddha

"Everything goes and everybody needs help
To get to the next, respect all sects"

But as I came down
And regained normal focus
To myself I say
Were those thoughts real or really bogus?

FELIPE COLÓN (aka CEE-LO)

Haiku

Few drops trickle down my cheek
Oh, beautiful autumn day! Leaves of every color
and the reality of my cage.

No Tears

In mid-July, on a hot Saturday morning around nine o'clock, you and your boy Tobi are coming back from Moyo's, the corner bodega, with a few of your boys—remember that? You are standing next to Tobi like you always did, rolling a blunt as you waited to cross the intersection of Beach and Oak Streets. Tobi is yo' dogg, he's from the block and your brothers Oso and Gabi are his little crimies. Tobi has lots of respect in the hood, Sun put that flame to many men in these streets. You look up to him. The two others are his sons, who you stay disrespecting because you know their true nature.

As you cross the street and make it to the center of Beach Street, a black '85 Monte Carlo comes to a stop right next to Tobi. A masked man slides half of his body out the passenger door window and pulls out what you know to be a .357 Smith and Wesson revolver, and in a very quick motion lets off two shots to Tobi's forehead. You feel something wet hit your face and shirt. You feel like running, but you know better. The masked man looks dead at your eyes and all you can say is: You gonna pay for that, homeboy! But he just slides his body back into the car and takes off.

You look down to the ground and see your boy with his wig split back and his brains out the back of it as your brother Oso, who heard the shots, comes out from his apartment and carries Tobi out of the street and over to the sidewalk. Everyone comes out to see what's happened. Tobi's mother is screaming and crying and so is everyone else in the block, yet you cannot shed a tear. You feel nothing. You go home, smoke the blunt he gave you to roll, and take a shower to wash his blood from your face. Still no tears.

This is real talk. It happened in July 1990. I was only nine, and Tobi was sixteen. One of many more I was to see fall victim to my first love.

Twenty-one years! And still never a tear.

I see how lost I was as a young star. I was in love with my very own self-destruction and worst enemy, my lower thoughts. See, the streets are what we make them, and I know I have always known that, I just never knew myself as I do now. Allah made the streets his school in Mecca for children like the one I used to be, so they wouldn't shed no tears.

I look to do the same with no shame, no tears, and best of all, no fear.

Who I Love

I love those who further my education and lead me to a better under-
standing of life.
I love she who birthed me into physical existence and cradled me
like the moon does a star.
I love the sun because he made me in the image of his reflection, a
life-giving light.
I love my family, although they are blind to their true self.
I love all the earths in my universe, for they are the soil of my seeds,
and although they are
        secondary, to life they are most necessary.
I love loyalty and respect.
I love the strong and the meek.
I love the wise poor righteous teachers dropping bombs in the street
corners to destroy evil.
I love knowledge, for it manifests itself through me in the form of
GOD to show and prove I am
        supreme.

Good Old Days

From selling fresh fish in Bayamon
to counting red, yellow, green, blue,
purple, and fuchsia-colored dollars in the
small streets of Holyoke, Mass.
Mother and father always making something
out of nothing without derailing from a
righteous path.
Big metal can of peanut butter with no jelly,
powder-blue box of milk,
Kate's Kitchen Lunches,
I used to love to have.

These are the things I miss about my past,
good old days,
memories that didn't last.

LATONE JAMES

A Christmas Story

You wake up to the sound of the rain hitting your window. Beads of sweat drip down your forehead onto your blood-colored silk pillowcase. You jump to your feet and realize that all of your clothes are off except for your white satin boxer shorts. You look to your left and see a figure in your bed wrapped in a plush white bedcover.

Slowly, you start to regain control of your memory and the events that led up to this moment. You retrace your memory to the night before. The meeting at the roundtable, where five grown men rehearsed their strategies on how to manipulate the mean streets of one of Connecticut's most dangerous cities.

After the meeting, the Christmas party. Looking back at the figure wrapped in the plush white bedcover, a deep smile sets in.

You walk to the bathroom to rinse your face. In the mirror you notice yourself. As your eyes meet your own gaze, you know that the life you've been living is dangerous, ruthless, even merciless. As you look at your reflection in the mirror you know that the fire that burns inside you is among the most powerful.

You are of average height, skin as yellow as a tropical fish, bald head, and eyes as black as a forest cave. The power you have mastered is of deceit and force. Your smile is virgin and your humor switches—at times it's of proper etiquette and education, at other times it's street slang—letting you fit into any ethnic background.

You focus your memory on the Christmas party, where you met Apollonia. Skin as gold as the 4:45 sunset and a body like a dark angel. She's beautiful, but you know she's just a golddigga' trying to come up. You also know that one of the other four bosses sic'd her on you to try to establish his dominance.

Despite everything going on in your everyday life, today is the day you try to focus your attention on the foster care community, where for the last five years you've been donating money and toys to kids without fathers. You're ruthless, but you know how it feels to wake up on Christmas morning without gifts. You head back to the bedroom and lightly touch Apollonia on her backside while bending over to whisper in her ear that it's time for her to head home, unless she's up for the part of playing Mrs. Claus.

JOHN BREWER III

Museum

My life is filled with conspiracies,
fulfilled fantasies, piracy.
I'm just a street corner brother
and the media still won't give me no privacy,
society denying me,
presidents lying to me,
prisons confining me,
scientists providing me
with intentions of silencing me,
fearing that when I speak the masses are minding me,
so they undermine my methods,
dig up graveyards to discredit my message,
I'm just a street corner brother.
It's because of you today's youth are self-destructive.
Yeah, right, like they can't see
that our leaders are reckless,
they blatantly disrespect us
by feeding us the illusion
that lavishness is inside a car or a necklace.
I'm just a street corner brother
and the media still won't give me no privacy.
They speak on my fetishes,
my cultural ideologies and sexual preferences,
like they really know what my preference is.
Is it weed, dust, coke, life, heroin, or prescribed medicine?
Does she have to be black, white, or Hispanic,
pro, chicken, or heaven sent,
real feminine or more toward mannish?

Excuse me, there goes a heroine—
pardon me, love.
But I'm just a street corner brother
and your classism, I can't stand it.
This is my life and your access has not been granted.
Perceptions, perceptions, perceptions.
My vision is obstructed by erected structures
of buildings, fences, even trees
trying to limit my perception
of life and death, love and hate, lust and passion.
Now that I'm not trying to see
I refuse to give up my aspirations and dreams.
Imagination is powerful, it allows me to escape
and rebuild reality.

8/2005 till 9/2011

The sky was bright blue, sun shining brightly on that beautiful summer day. You sat there on the freshly painted park bench, dressed in your Sassoon jeans, jelly sandals, and "Fight the Power" tank top, with your Nefertiti earrings and your hair wrapped up.

Yes, you were, and still are, sexy.

You were watching the young brothers messing with the girls jumping double dutch and the little children chasing the ice cream truck when out of nowhere you heard a man screaming at the top of his lungs—at whom, you didn't know, until you saw your beautiful long-lost sister coming at what seemed to be 100 miles-per-hour, her long, flowing locks ripping through the firmament, her arms swinging and throwing things viciously. You ran and hid, ducking for cover behind the blue postal box, holding tightly onto its legs as she continued on her rampage.

You think to yourself, "Did Walker put his hand on her? Did he pollute her with some of his poisonous venom, knowing that she's pregnant? Was he deliberately trying to kill her baby or babies?"

"Help! Help! Help!" Robert's family screamed. "Help! Help! Help!" your friends yelled. "Mama's seizing! John-Boy's bleeding!"

As your sister calmed down, you reached up and gained balance and strength, asking Shay if she's all right. "Where's my baby? Where's my baby?" she yelled while you helped her look for little Keisha. You couldn't help but notice Tyrone James and Leroy lying next to you, on top of a crying baby. But they were bleeding from the head—gunshot wounds—and the emergency response team was off saving animals.

You cried—I cried, too, as I continued to fight my way to the grocery store to find food, and soon the police arrested me for what they called stealing and we call surviving. You became angry and screeched out, "You hypocrites are doing the same thing!" and fainted. I yelled "Help! HELP! Where's FEMA?" and you came through, saying, "Saving a dog." Then suddenly you had a similar outburst, ripping out all the IV needles the paramedics had put in you, causing more destruction. Lights out, six years later.

A Memory

Mommy licked her fingers and wiped my snotty nose and crusty
eyes at the bus stop.
I was hung from a tree by my wrists,
whooped like a slave
and kissed by the flyest queens,
rocked Calvin Kleins and hand-me-down jeans.
Don't get me to reminiscing about our Playboy re-enactments—
I'm talking about the channel, dogg, not the magazine.
And this was in grades 2 and 3,
we're humping humping humping humping machines,
dressed to the nines with ol' dad and his fly ol' rags
drinking Ballantine Ale in his LTD with the fly ol' rag,
diamond in the back, sunroof top digging the scene with my
gangsta lean.
Yeah, I was sippin' too,
True.
It all happened on the Bishop side of the Square Park,
all of my memories are both bright and dark.
So while reflecting, this is where I'll stop
right at the start:
Mommy licked her fingers and wiped my snotty nose and crusty
eyes at the bus stop.

Listen (I Should've)

Mind-blowing scores of football numbers,
I slumbered until the hammer clapped.
The slug, it missed me, or I missed it,
until I saw a friendly on her back.
What you crying for? Stand strong.
It ain't over, I'll be back!
I'm standing in degrees of 32.
At least that's what he said,
and he said she said and he said,
and now me digi in this revolving door.
Why didn't you tell me about the life you foreseen,
The pictures clearly painted by the so-called Gee's before me,
and explain the contrastic missions of
Angela, David, Fred, and Huey Pee,
Father Allah and Just-I-Cee?
Equality—what is that?
Why didn't you tell me about the visions
or the essence of a dream becoming a reality?
Or did you and I missed it?
Or did it miss me because as I reflect
a speck comes back to me?
Damn, I've been committing blasphemy,
living in vain;
God—dishonoring your good name,
in the illusion of fame for some trim,
pain pain pain,
lynchings,
they hung Auntie's man and now I'm shooting him,
my closest kin. How can I win?
Will you please tell me,

or did you and I refused to listen,
distracted by the game money,
you up at bat and I'm pitching,
for what? An imaginary plaque,
war stories,
how social studies bored me so I slept
while Jesus wept,
and good old Master Harvey
taught his chil'ren to study my social economy.
Why do I bottom feed?
Why didn't you tell me about your grandfather's legacy
and his father's specialty?
Of course I'll never forget the jewels you bought me,
But I wish you would've taught me more
about the lineage that makes me
instead of the turmoil and strife suffered
that you continuously see on the face of me.
I wish you would've taught me about me.
Maybe you did.
Damn, I wish I would've listened.

IVAN DIAZ

The Room I Wake Up In

For over seventeen years I have woken up in this lifeless, dreary belly of the beast that never seems to digest its human nourishment. My senses come to life before dawn, gathering their individual thoughts and information like a rank of soldiers assessing the battlefield in contemplation for the subjugation of the enemy.

My ears register the monotonous sound of the air system mingling with that of a fan, akin to the sound coming from a long dark tunnel with no end in sight, the humming sound echoing in the distance like that of an old war plane that approaches at a steady pace but never arrives.

As I open my eyes in the dark, my vision momentarily falters in the murky fog of my sleepy state. As the seconds tick on by and the lenses of my periscope begin to focus, the windows of my soul draw in an already familiar scene.

A waft of sweet-scented Egyptian oil flows freely in the air of the confined cubicle, yet undeterred, as free as a bird in the open skies overlooking a canyon. There I lie in a brief trance looking on, with an empty basket of thoughts.

I conjure up my strength and a rush of power shoots through my arms into my hands. The sensors at the tips of my fingers register the terrain, like mine sweepers on the sandy beach of Normandy. I leap like a cat onto what appears to be a sea of ice. Walking across the brazen cold, I come to an oasis, where I am greeted by a splash of cold, soothing water in the face of a hot and dry Saharan desert. The coolness of what tastes like Schnapps on ice fills my dry cotton mouth, bringing all my senses back to life in a familiar ritual performed before the morning sun as it rises over the horizon to look into the eyes of this monster.

Finally, all my senses recoil as the sun climbs higher onto its pedestal. I rise again like a phoenix to face another day in the belly of this beast. It is a recurring play as I awaken from my sleep to realize that what I have just described in metaphors is not a dream, it is the prison cell I live in.

DAVID KENDRICK

To Miles Davis

Frederick Douglass, Malcolm, Martin, Train, Jimmie, Monk
I thought about them first, Miles
But you have touched me in recent days
Since they have been kind of blue
A grown man wearing a shirt full of tears
I can't explain nothing to these jive turkeys
That shiver in their own fears

Cat Daddy, you dated Cicely Tyson
Is she the one who gave you the bitches' brew?
The way you played that trumpet, those notes flew
Miles . . . those sounds danced on my ear drums for weeks
I stayed in my cocoon, I didn't want to speak
When I exited back into the world, it was like the birth of the cool
I had my swagger, slick! I mean, Miles
You took me to school with style, you dig?

Like Hog Maul, Mustard, and Collard Greens
Inside of a bullpen full of inmates. Jazz. It's funky
My heart goes out to you because
Most of your band died as junkies
Couldn't let loose that monkey
They was bad, though
Especially Train!
I wish he didn't tap those veins
and kept playing that sax
That had the women on the chitlin circuit spinning . . . hoppin'
Fingers poppin', corn bread with brown gravy soppin'

And Monk, he was eclectic and all, tapping those black and white keys
Max Roach bouncing those sticks on those drums
Man, I wish I was there to get some . . . of that!

Miles, I'm only writing this and all
Because my crew is dying inside of these prison walls
Where talent falls by the waist
Somehow I heard you say in your low, raspy voice
Cat Daddy, pick up your face
What those jive turkeys do
Don't have to be your case
Just write, slick, just write . . .
Yeah!

My Wedding Day

I wake up in the morning
knowing I am more than beautiful
Hmmm – extravagant, quite virtuous
elegant, definitely stunning, pretty in anything I wear
I can be bald, have an afro, long hair
wig or nest
just gorgeous beyond the looker
I do not dress to impress
I can be naked and called a saint
an artist's Mona Lisa
a photographer's Marilyn Monroe
Put me in a magazine or on a stage
I can sing to the president off-pitch and all
shatter Cinderella's slipper at the ball
and run off with her prince
dashing, jumping over a fence
falling, laughing, into his arms
I will challenge him with a riddle
his face poised, confused, amazed at my wisdom
He will call me Solomon's daughter
Confucius' granddaughter
shouting to the world:
Pave the streets with gold!
Line them with rose petals!
Chocolates, diamonds, and pearls
to the end of the road!
He would not let me shiver or feel the slightest of cold
I will feel the warmth of many furs, minks, foxes, chinchillas, and lynx
the thick hair of a bear
or the mane of a lion, King of the Jungle!

I will soon
be his queen
a sensation to the nation
My people will be in awe, mesmerized
as I walk down the aisle
and he will catch me with his eyes
and take me as his prize
and I will say
I do.

ANTHONY BRUNETTI

The Heavy Bag

The heavy bag that was brand new.
The heavy bag that was hard like rock.
The heavy bag that stood firm against a child's punches.
The heavy bag I loved but physically abused.
The heavy bag that became soft like cotton.
The heavy bag I punched.
The heavy bag I kicked.
The heavy bag I elbowed.
The heavy bag that saw my best days.
The heavy bag that felt the wrath of my worst.
The heavy bag that never hit back—the ultimate listener.
The heavy bag that was always there for me.
The heavy bag that was hit by a would-be champion.
The heavy bag that took all that abuse but was deprived by the
government the privilege to be the punching bag of a world champion.
The heavy bag I no longer punch.
The heavy bag I miss.
My heavy bag.

Untitled

A man is sitting on his bed, meditating. It is dark and quiet. There is no one else around.

The man sits still, trance-like. With my third eye I see a brilliant golden aura surrounding and continually emanating from him.

He begins to float, levitating a few feet above his bed. But he is unfazed by this. Oblivious to what's occurring in the physical, his aura of golden light gets brighter and brighter. He is in perfect harmony with the universe, completely cognizant of his divine self.

Unbreakable Bond

Our love is divine,
Our bond unbreakable,
Not even Excalibur could rend us asunder.

The whale of Jonah has swallowed me,
But I will pry its jaws open and slay Leviathan
To hold you in my arms the rest of my days.

Your company is my heaven,
Your form that of a goddess.

You are perfection personified,
God's beauty in motion.

The One and Only

I'm proud to be the undisputed king.
I regret some of the lives I ended.
I'm proud to have defeated multiple enemies by myself.
I regret some of the destruction I've caused.
(But hey, I'm destructive by nature—some of it was intentional,
some inadvertent.)
I'm proud they still haven't figured out how to kill me.
I regret letting the children of my frenemy bind me up.
I'm proud to have successfully cooperated with others in some of
the battles I've fought.
I regret not being the hero earlier in my life.
I'm proud of having been made an official ambassador of Japan.
I regret not destroying all the prisons yet.
I'm proud of my powerful radiation blast, my spikes, my terror-invoking roar, and my ability to withstand atomic bombs and nuclear attacks.
I regret that there are people who don't like my movies.
I'm proud and honored to be the one and only
KING OF MONSTERS.

DANYELL PICKETT

Untitled

I sit here thinking that I finally found her
A girl who makes me feel love when I am around her
But I am afraid that it won't last
But is that too much to ask?
The empty spot in my heart is no longer vacant
I hope the love we share can make it
I'll give 100% to make sure each moment
Is spent intimate.

MICHAEL STREATER

The Sneakers

The sneakers with the fat laces.
The sneakers that dodged the police.
The sneakers that got me money.
The sneakers that took your money.
The sneakers I played ball with.
The sneakers that put Five-O on my trail.
The sneakers that took my girl.
The sneakers that rolled the best Eel.
The sneakers that dodged the police.
The sneakers that talked away my pain.
The sneakers that were always true to the game.
The sneakers that brought me the gun.
The sneakers that would never let me run.
The sneakers that reared my first child.
The sneakers that held me down while I was away.
The sneakers I got flicks from.
The sneakers that are called dad by my son.
The sneakers with the worn-down sole.
The sneakers that always take on water through the hole.
The sneakers that are always out of date.
The sneakers with multiple cases out of state.
The sneakers that have no name.
The sneakers that bring me nothing but shame
Are the sneakers I'll wear for the rest of my life
    Because they're so comfortable.

The Meeting

You notice the spider web silk,
strains of hair blown like the flag of a ship
entering the port of a lost isle
to a lost child.
She turns toward you with mirrored image eyes
that are shaped like brown diamonds
on the surface of butterscotch sand,
and says, "What?"
Now the ball is in your hands.
Your throat constricts
like the pressure of the world's largest anaconda
as memories of your forty-year living coma,
death's aroma,
doesn't provide the word of wisdom that
each day of her life you've longed to convey.
You respond, "Nothing."
What else could you say?
You continue to stare and observe
the belt strap across her body,
holding her as a father would his child,
protecting, caring, loving,
as the fragile being thunders along in the sports utility vehicle
at speeds that border on the doors of sound,
tires barely touching the ground.
A small flicker, like eye lint,
causes you to peer upward at
the reflection of one son and daughter,
causes you to rear up,
they are as unknown as the variable in an algebra equation
that are new beginnings and roads to salvation,

asleep in the back like angels on vacation.
The choices of yesteryear have given fruit to new situations.
How will you do it?
What type of life can you make when the reality is
that you are broker than a glass house in an earthquake
and hungrier than an Ethiopian
fasting during the month of Ramadan?
And you have only this beautiful woman to lean upon.
Your memories of past choices paint an image on your face,
of life on the run with multiple cases out of state.
The joy that you chased but in life you never had.
You're snapped back to reality by words you never knew
as the person next to you says,
"Dad, you know I love you."
So, my question to you all is:
what's a dad to do?

You Don't Know Me

You don't know me
My name carries no sound
My life is seen with eyes that are blind
My yesterdays and tomorrows are the heres and nows
I walk the roads in life that are not part of my plans
I was carried as a baby, crawled as a child
And long to see the days as a man

You don't know me
My face has no shape
I'm grown enough to make choices
But only realize when it's too late
That my friends and foes are one and the same
All's fair in love and war
And the life we call the game

You don't know me
But I'm just like you
Constantly confused about what to do
Who to trust and what to be
Confused because no one ever really understands me
A dark spot in the light
Or awareness in a void
A crippled man walking
A deaf man who hears a noise
My life is not perfect but it's all I've got
Standing alone in an empty room
Afraid of choosing the wrong spot
So I laugh at my tears and I smile at the pain
Of how I dream when I'm awake of planting flowers in the rain

Joy is just a word and love is much less so
Failure a daily dish so I long to never grow
I'm the tallest of all the trees
My sight is very clear
My heart is overgrown with who gives a what
And I don't cares

But you don't know me
So don't waste your time
From a world of "Yo, that's my man right there"
To a choice of who's going to do the time
See, Dad was there when he wanted to be
Yet he never laid eyes on me
We never played catch
We never shot ball
He never told me how great I'd be
My ups and downs were rights and lefts
Looking from face to face
My ins and outs were highs and lows
Moving from place to place
Through all and all I stand firm and tall
And can look you square in the eye
Because you don't know me
And despite this fact you might wonder why

You don't know me
It's all because I don't know me either.

Ode to Water

Easily forgotten
yet forever present,
a lady that demands respect,
always faithful,
like the loving embrace
of a mother
that can crush
the mountains
like the wrath of a god.
Clean,
pure,
the tears that wash
away the sorrows
of lost dreams and tomorrows.
You are the intrinsic part
of all things
but refuse to be held
in check, like the wind
through the blades of a large fan.
Who can travel anywhere?
You can,
through the earth,
like the veins and arteries
you deliver life and refinement.
The Nile, Tigris, Mississippi, Pee Dee,
Hudson, your names are many.
You are the home
that supplies,
through the space of all time
you survive.

At times this oven
heats up,
blazes,
enflamed, as the sun
licks the surface of our land.
You are a warrior
battling the flames, the blaze,
the sound of your fighting
like a pit of hungry snakes,
takes form as the heat
runs to the heavens,
misty, raising steam,
seeking forgiveness
as it joins your armies.

You appear in the heavens,
millions of pure white butterflies
descend like a cover
laid upon a resting child
by a loving parent.
And yet with all of your care
you are to be feared.
From above you appear
as millions of angry punches
breaking, bursting, smashing,
you open up as the world's
largest waterfall,
flooding the land,
sweeping, pushing, dragging
any and all in your path.
All that you give

you can take away.
Easily forgotten
yet forever present.
And I thought you should know
that I'm always thinking about
you.
H2O ...

IAN T. COOKE

Untitled

Pitch black night illuminated by amber yellow security lights in intervals. I hop the low stone wall, the top few stones loose. The still night air pierced by the grinding of stone on stone, and then disaster: one falls crashing down like deep bass drums.

And silence again, briefly.

A few steps into the yard light, steps on soft grass and the black shadow in the light becomes apparent. No time for retreat; I've come too far. The shadow moves and his collar rings, metal on metal. My only hope for escape: the chain holding him back.

I know the big Doberman well, and he knows me. Our relationship goes way back. Every time I try to sneak through his yard, he's there.

The deep, throaty bark rings out once, a warning, and I shiver with the memory of my father yelling at me, that baritone full of strength and hatred.

I don't know if the Doberman hates me. He's just doing what he knows. I'm in his world.

The second bark precedes the chase. I hate the chase. I'm frozen in fear, yet my legs move out of necessity. I'm so close to the curb, the neutral zone—public domain. Does he know this? Can I make it? He's so close.

In Memoriam

I walk through trees for hours—miles.
The trees open into sunlight.
Once I step into the clearing, I am alone.

There are no trees, no wilderness, just sky above.
The blue sky is freedom.
The clearing is silence.

A solitary boulder
Stands at the border,
And I climb atop it.

Up above, here, I can see for miles all around.
Up above, I am closer to freedom.
I will stay here until I die.

Flying, Part II

. . . and with a little hop he's off—off the ledge and into the air, falling at first, gravity only. Then with a flourish of his azure plumage and an upward warm air current, aloft, floating down more than falling. A tiny flap of his wings and up—flap flap flap—up up up— and he's flying above the trees, above the rocks, above it all. The sky is so clean, blue, free. And then clouds. At first the clouds are fluffy and white; soon enough, gray and black. He sees a flash—lightning. A strike nearby, then another, and another. He's hit, struck, falling, falling, smoking, back to earth, straight to the ground, beautiful feathers floating down, fallen everywhere. But he's not dead, not after falling, He twitches on the ground. Wings tattered, beak dulled, feathers dirtied, smoking. But alive, he can barely move. He's only thinking about flying.

Who Is This?

We pull up on a little gravel parking area. He's nervous, maybe apprehensive, sitting next to me driving. The place looks all right from the outside. Dark brown clapboards in a seventies style. Detached townhouses are decent enough.

We get to the door. He goes in. I pause at the threshold, noticing the smell. Rather, the stench. Its layers of putrid eking into my pores. I reluctantly step inside, and the most pervasive smell envelops me. Dank, old standing water. Mildew. But *old* mildew, like it was aged in a barrel. Then the cat piss smell takes over. It makes me retch. I notice piles of petrified droppings in the corners of the room. Like the cat—or, more likely, the *cats*—were marking the boundaries of their domain.

He disappears up the narrow flight of stairs and returns when he realizes I'm not in tow. Perhaps a look of disgust has washed over my face. He feels obligated to give me an explanation, or what would be the start of the whole story.

"We got to live here on the cheap since we're fixing the place up."
Could've fooled me.

"Couldn't get the cat smell out of the floor so we stripped up the carpets and painted over the wood."

He gives the impression that he actually believes this is an improvement. I pause a bit too long, not so much speechless as aghast with all of this.

He leads me upstairs. There is a desk and a bed. Most of the stuff is already gone. It's a good thing it's daytime—there aren't any lights. No lamps, no fixtures, no bulbs that I can see. Almost as if scavengers have gone through the place to loot for copper wiring or anything not nailed down. Some light cascades into the window. There is no dust, to my surprise. There are, however, little eddies of fur in the corners. I have yet to see a cat.

127

"All right," he says, "let's take out the box spring and the frame. We can get the desk last. It's more of a pain in the ass."

Fine by me. Let's get this over with.

We load a few things in the trailer easily enough. One more trip. I beat him back upstairs, not as any sort of sibling rivalry or anything conscious, I guess it's enthusiasm for getting this over with.

I start pulling out the desk drawers, thinking I'll lighten the load of the wooden behemoth. I notice a little cellophane wrapper in the top drawer. Think nothing of it. Well into my teens, I've seen him smoking for at least ten years. I open another drawer to pile on the floor. Another trove of paraphernalia. Bic lighters and condom wrappers. *Something to be said for that.* And as I set the drawer down he comes into the bedroom doorway, pauses abruptly. I notice this in my peripheral vision, and then I notice another baggie in the drawer. A small Zip-loc bag too small to be of use for anything normal. Almost like the Barbie and Ken version of a sandwich bag. It's empty, but sort of filmed with a white haze.

I look up and away. He steps to the desk and tells me to grab the other end. As I turn to pick it up, he reaches down, palms the baggie, and secrets it into his front jeans pocket. *Subtle.*

We heft the desk to the top of the stairs without a word. It's sort of hard jockeying it around that weird corner that the top of all stairs have, where it meets the hallway. But we manage to get it around and I let the desk punch a dot-dot-dot of Morse code in the drywall on our way down. I certainly don't care about this place or this desk.

At the trailer we stow everything away. I don't go back inside.

He comes out a final time and we drive off. I don't look at him, don't speak to him. He glances sidelong at me once or twice but never manages to speak.

When we get home, I get out with absolutely zero pretense of helping him unload this crap. He just sits there in the driver's seat, door ajar, as I walk toward the house.

"You won't say anything, will you?"

I half turn and stop and think about this. *What did he just say?* I walk back to the front of the car, five paces, and a world of difference.

"What?"

"It's not as bad as it seems. I mean, you know, it's *nothing*."

I look at this man I used to admire, used to idolize, and in an instant sitting below me on that car seat, he is the child.

"I don't have anything to say, not to them and not to you ... Who *are* you?"

My Mother's Hands

Looking at a painting, I see the hands of the artist.

I see my mother with a brush and think about what those hands have created. The times when even as a child I'd watch her sitting at an easel and marvel at how blank canvas could be transformed.

I look at my hand grasping a brush in the same loose, whimsical manner that she once did. The tender skin on the back of my hand looks like the spider web cracking of broken glass, delicate and ready to shatter.

A speck of paint drips down and color seeps into the little cracks, and I feel old.

My mother's hands, now old and wrinkled, replace mine, and I dwell on my mortality. How much longer can I grasp the brush? What can I create with my time?

With these hands I can be immortal.

Art lasts forever.

Regrets

Yeah, forget you,
I have none.
Regret is a waste of time,
It's not for me . . .
That's why I always stay busy.

You're like the reaper
Looming at my door,
Waiting for a lull,
And then you kill my joy.

I spend my whole day running away.
All those memories,
All that I could be,
And all the while you're chasing after me.

How do you think that makes me feel?
I'm tired.
Everything that's lost, gone, never to be . . .
But as soon as I close my eyes,
You're there . . . nagging at me.

If only it were true.
I keep telling myself I have no regrets.
So why the hell can't I get away from you?

Will Be, Can Be, Is

You and I will go out under the stars,
It will be autumn and the evening air crisp, not biting,
You'll walk out to that field,
The one that's luscious and emerald by day,
Then it will be almost obsidian in its darkness,
but shimmering the reflective sparkle,
You'll stand out like the white queen adjacent the black king,
poised for conquest
But serene in your stillness,
Then your hair will catch a faint breeze
And platinum strands of starlight will waft about restlessly,
We'll lie on that cool, cushioning carpet
With body heat radiating the meadow,
Our feet pointing skyward and your head juxtaposed
inches from mine,
Eons' starlight reflecting glassy in your eyes
As our moment's still breath will fade into eternity.

Out of Focus

There's a mirror near my door. I walk by it every time I walk out that door. I see a blur move past that reflective silver. I distract myself.

The blur is too dark, or too light, or too blurry, and it feels foreign. If I didn't recognize the shape in the mirror I stop and look. I don't walk out that door; I just stand there looking.

Maybe I expect someone else to start looking back. Maybe I don't even think about it. One of those things that just happens or just is.

The mirror is a strange thing, an ode to vanity that's become necessity . . . for some reason. *How do I look*? turns into *How do I feel*?

This mirror by the door doesn't make sense to me. It's not in the right place. When I walk by, I'm only half there. Half a shoulder. Half a face. Half a man.

The image reflected back at me is still blurry; only when I get real close does it come into focus. By then I lose the big picture, and the person looking back could be anyone. Faint hairs and pores in my nose. Only when I see the eyes do I see familiarity.

I try to stare at one eye at a time, but for some reason I can't see the detail. I can't help but think that if I could focus on that one eye—either one—it would be like staring into the soul.

Not looking, but actually seeing—I don't know what that would be like. I don't know if I truly want that. The man behind the mirror reaches out and draws you in, and you get lost, lost in all those things you are but were never meant to see.

If I stand here and stare long enough, I expect to feel recognition, I expect the whole image to come into focus, I expect it all to make sense.

What I Want My Words to Do to You
or, The Reason for Apathy

I want my words to touch you,
because if they didn't, what would be the point?
I want my words to grab you and hold you,
because there's nothing worse than boredom.

When this happens, I want you to feel what I feel.
I want you to feel what I felt while writing them.
More importantly, I want you to feel what I felt
experiencing those experiences.

And I want you to feel pain,
the pain of my life.

I want you to feel heartache,
the shards of a broken heart piercing like shattered plate glass.

I want you to feel sorrow,
the sort of sorrow that keeps you in bed after your alarm goes off,
the kind of sorrow that makes you avoid people and eye contact,
the kind of sorrow that makes the ground more inviting than the sky

I want you to feel these things with my words,
because to feel them in person would leave you broken, like me.

Maybe I want you to feel apathy,
because to feel anything else is folly.

Maybe you should feel nothing,
because that's what I feel now, and it's the only way I survive.

Maybe you should know that every day makes me worse, not better. My words tell the truth of how it was, but not so much how it is.

If my words told you how it is, you'd stop reading.

Portrait by Ian T. Cooke

Heartbeat

My heart beats
beats – beats – skip – beats. Stop –
The world goes black and euphoria sets in,
a brain deprived of oxygen,
the simplest thought survives.
Love must be in there somewhere deep,
the inner recesses of the gray matter,
where the blood pools even when
the heart stops beating.
A jolt – I feel . . . pain.
A sharp – anger instantaneous – electric –
Stop.
Another jolt – beat – beat.
The pain hurts and helps.
Resuscitate, breath, pump, stop.
Once more because she doesn't give up.
Pump. Breath. Jolt.
Beat.
The euphoria's gone. Just the pain remains.
But my eyes stay closed.
I try to retain
not pain.
Blink, beat . . .
Light.

Portrait by Ian T. Cooke

Key Ring

You signify freedom. Not freedom—liberty.

You're easily forgotten, left in coat pockets, purses, fallen in between couch cushions, left in the dish by the door or on the dresser with the spare change.

I had a set made of plastic dangled in my face as a toddler, bright, multi-colored.

When I got my first key ring, I sought out any key to call my own. Errant padlocks became mine by virtue of their key on my ring.

A house key. Another house key, for the door no one uses.

It would be a few more years until you got your own car key, that true symbol of freedom.

By the time I was a teenager, you looked like something a school janitor would carry, laden with so many keys for so many locks, too heavy with keys to be practical.

But that bulk signified more . . . importance than pragmatism.

Locks sometimes protect secrets.

Locks for valuables, locks for doors.

A few short years later and I had lost you.

Not in a couch cushion.

I lost you as I lost everything.

Freedom. Liberty.

I don't have a key ring of my own now, though I see them every day.

I *can't* have you, because you mean freedom.

And you keep me here.

Every day.

Forever.

A SMILE. TOUCH. A KISS. SAVOR EACH. GOOD MORNING I

EVERY DAY
THE SUN SHINES OVER THE
HORIZON. A WARM EMBRACE.
THE DARKNESS FADES AWAY.
AND IT'S ALL NEW. ONCE AGAIN.

Dust to Dust

I was there when you were robust.
Now you're not.
Once a warm, embracing balloon frame with plenty of padding,
Now you're hollow,
Just a shell.

I think of how it was always a work in progress.
I still see piles of materials stacked neatly,
As if ready to build.
Now, they're sodden with chemicals and moisture and mold.

I walk through this strange earthen swell that is at times familiar
and comforting,
While equally acrid and disconcerting.
These once great bones are covered in a thin film of ash.
When I touch it, my fingers go black, like I'm putting on war paint.

Some of those bones are brittle with high heat osteoporosis,
Some are just faking illness, still formidable.
I take the chance to climb this skeletonized staircase
From once-a-foyer into once-a-hallway through once-a-doorway
Into my bedroom.
It will always be my bedroom.
That wall always had a poster and the corner a nightstand
Replete with a glow in the dark clock.
Part of my room is now in my basement,
My basement that's now a murky swimming pool of flotsam and
encroaching nature.

There's suddenly a deep groan within, and a crack,
A splintering gunshot in the otherwise barren silence,
Like great glaciers calving ice age melt into an unknowable abyss.
I feel movement, an instability
I dare not test.
Fate and logic dictate that this once great home is
Closer now to the ground than the sky,
And unlike the phoenix, it won't rise again.

It's time for me to say goodbye.

About Time

Write about life. Not your life, the state's life.

Write about the day you got sentenced, because your life is no longer yours.

Write about property.

Write about belongings and possession.

Once the state has your life, you're a number, an entry in a ledger. You're property, not a person.

Write about the people in that room.

Write about the judge and the attorneys. These are the ones who dabble with numbers as arbitrary as the clouds in the sky.

Write about those years, decades, the time that means nothing to those people—nothing to anyone but you.

Write about reflection and recognition.

Write about how long it takes for years to become reality, because it doesn't set in, not right away, it sets like concrete; at first, it's fluid and changeable, then it hardens and forms and becomes permanent.

Write about time.

Write about doing time, your time and their time.

Write about the passage of time and the experience.

Write about time.

Because it's about time for a change.

MYSTERY

Love That Was Not Love

What do I seek? For I am sorely distressed, being blind and bound by the passion of my own flesh. I, Samson, whom you know as the man who could defeat many men—thousands—now I am felled by the love of a harlot, my enemy's greatest trick. You would think me a fool to reveal the secret that made my arm amongst men stronger than steel. But you do not know Delilah, whose soft hands are so gentle, but so easily can break your will. A fool indeed, beguiled by a force unseen, burning in my flesh. Under a spell, it would seem, but now lost in my heart. I am torn, for this affair was not love, only passion disguised behind the feathers of a dove. I cannot cut off my heart to you, but I am now at my end. By these two pillars, you, Delilah, the woman who has wounded and deceived my heart, will know my displeasure before eternity begins . . .

NATHANIEL O. CHAMBERS

Untitled

A poem composed in celebration of ur birth
Essentially bet on kismet, for all it's worth
Not sure whether I'm early or belated
All I know is that, unfortunately, internally
I long 4 my love sent from above
Yet I'm significantly segregated
Didn't want to disturb ur studies so I deferred these poems
Perfect practical poetry, predicting pliable present unknowns
Regardless—do my best to express, nevertheless, while I sincerely say
Recompense, regularly repeated love lines, day after day
Like the sun, U were my bright light, removing the stale, pale
darkness within
That's that—über-legit once we decided to commit and begin
There was no chance, or circumstance 4 a loss, only a continuous win
U allowed me to reach new unknown heights, peaking planets,
like Mars
Especially since ur kisses would send me so far beyond these skies
and stars
Miss that lunar eclipse
Parting and indulging in ur lips
Ur truly beyond stellar and out of this dimension
And I must mention U will always be worthy of all my affection
Girl, do doubt, no question that ride should never subside
Girl, no deceit, it was short yet sweet for us 2 meet—quite the feat
Grasping ur hand, being ur man, there's no measure, was a pleasure
I'd love 2 repeat
Enjoying my pampering clutch, w/ U as my boo I was all set

Tender touch after touch, grandeur and ur feedback assure u will never forget
I'm that unordinary dude, passionately providing unselfish servitude
Prose and plows is all Nate the Great knows
Yet no test, Sassy Cassie's the best I've had by far
I perfect dialect and battle 'cause love is war
Effortlessly, so plain to see Cassie was the only one for me
U are Native American sovereignty, royalty, like kings and queens
I thank God for blessing me with an opportunity
To spend diving time with the woman of my dreams
Consequently, it was destiny, the moment we held an embrace
React—eye contact—followed by passionate making out, face to face
Had a new start and a college sweetheart—MXCC is the place
On the tablet of ur heart, save the most jocose times we shared
The entire world would stop when U returned my stare
Delight in eyesight, escalating each episode even more
Divinely deep dialogue devised daily when we used to explore
U quenched my thirst like a tall glass of organic juice
U were my fine wine and still are Danielle's beautiful papoose
U are her first true love, a soaring dove from above
Life-changing gift many adore, changing the world since "1994"
Never plain, prefer plotting parables permanently poetically insane
Know I will be strong if U move on, all I ask is that U don't sigh or cry
Time heals all—I always held ur hand so I wouldn't slip or fall
Let's start a clean slate, please be strong 2 and appreciate ur Great Nate.

BMX Lifestyle

Old, squeaky wood, try not to make noise as I turn on the light
So I can stomp as many roaches as possible—the 'hood's number
one endless fight
Hyper rev turbo FC35 and FD35 RX7 catalog
As I enter, smile, and glance at the KEI office coil-over brochure
Hoping when I move my BMX off the package the carbon fiber hood
won't fall to the floor
Getting around all these things on a daily basis
Try not to step over none of my things as I exit to see places
Don't slip on that valve grinding compound residue or the carbide
deburring bits
Ported and polished intake manifold, high-speed drill
Check and double-check the tape I used to keep the spare roll cage
tubing is holding together
Apexi blow-off valve and basic training picture—their worth has
no measure
Lastly, look at the ceiling fan that doesn't work and the swain tech
coating price guide
At least my street session won't be this cluttered, all I want to do is
get out and ride.

Christ's Soldier

First thing I notice is the khaki uniform
Gonna wear it for two and a half decades . . . dispatch non-comform-ity

You see, prior applicability and suitability was an ACU
with the 102nd Infantry

ACU is the abbreviation for Army Combat Uniform

Look into the mirror . . . visionary-glance
regardless of the circumstance

I was—and am still—a veteran
of the war on Iraq—not Afghan
Suddenly understand . . . although unplanned
have been Christ soldier from a boy to a man
My calling was a 56M
confident (ChapAss LOLZ) Chaplain-Assistant

Abruptly recall the
Soldier's Creed:
I am an American soldier
I am a warrior and member of a team
I serve the people of the United States and live the Army values
I will always place the mission first
I will never accept defeat I will never quit
I will never leave a fallen comrade
I will always maintain my arms my equipment and myself
I am an expert and I am a professional
I stand ready to deploy engage and destroy
the enemies of the United States of America in close combat

I am a guardian of freedom and the American way of life
I am an American soldier . . . HOOOAH!

The deployment to Iraq was life changing
I volunteered with the 192nd Military Police
for a detainee operations mission

Truly been on both sides of the fence
past and present tense
tense present
since I am locked up doing time in the present time

Would've had a pension doing these 25 years in the military
Would have been restrained or restricted to a limited area
Here or there share some snare somewhere beware
Tough stuff either way
Countdown to the day
By snatching a tray
Snatching a seat while I rock to my own beat
Chow! is surprisingly called the same name

Jinba Ittai No Longer

After I pumped gas . . . stepped inside.
All's manual in my Mazda . . . satisfied.
Inattentive Volvo driver t-boned me . . . Plow!
Devoured light, right into me . . . Collide!

I've got to make it to college somehow,
Cannot forget the sweat of my brow.
Damn diabolical dumbass dealt me a death blow!
Bad timing for an accident . . . especially now.

Didn't enter a ring . . . yet received TKO,
Destroyed a *jinba ittai* . . . truck and NCO,
Adrenaline was pumping . . . I'm beyond tense,
Were carried away by a repo.

His actions truly have no defense,
Idiot is an idiot . . . no coincidence.
Damage dealt, all at my expense,
Damage dealt, all at my expense.

The Truck

The truck that initially passed inspections flawlessly
The truck that was totaled and was rebuilt
The truck that turned from daily driver to daily drifter
The truck that had its power rack swapped out for a manual one
The truck that had its air conditioner removed for less clutter, weight
The truck that had all six windows open during summer and spring
The truck that took a hit of the Go Fast crack pipe and was never the same
The truck with all emissions removed
The truck with assorted vinyl vacuum caps in place of OEM ports
The truck with ceramic coated pacesetter open headers
The truck that didn't have a catalytic converter
The truck with DEI titanium exhaust-wrapped headers
The truck with a 2.5-inch bottle style resonator and straight pipe
The truck with a 2.5 Mandrel bent driver-side exit exhaust
The truck with blue polyurethane eBay exhaust hangers
The truck with 12-point chrome ARP intake and exhaust studs
The truck that ditched its stock carburetor
The truck that replaced it with an outlaw 38/38 Weber carburetor
The truck with an electric choke
The truck that had its grille hacked in order to fit a velocity stack with integrated intake tube from Weapon R
The truck with a universal open element breather on the valve cover
The truck with Blue Dash-6 Push-Loc hose plumbed into the intake manifold
The truck with a Jegs 2-row aluminum Ford-style radiator
The truck that used a folding KHE BMX tire to snugly mount the aforementioned radiator
The truck with its Mashimoto blue stainless steel hose kit
The truck that advanced its timing

The truck with an MSD high vibration blaster coil
The truck with NGK ceramic spark plugs
The truck with a cad-plated blaster coil bracket
The truck with Lucas oil additive installed with a funnel each gas pump
The truck that should have had an oil cooler installed
The truck that drifted in front of a state trooper and only received a warning
The truck that would hit its 110 mph top speed frequently
The truck that beat both a third generation Eclipse owner and his pride
The truck that out-cornered and outpaced an Acura RSX
The truck with a cracked windshield and equally cracked owner
The truck that lost on the highway to a Toyota Tacoma
The truck with no cup holders
The truck with soiled carpet from spilled milkshakes
The truck with S5 RX7 black and gray bucket seats
The truck with an FB RX7 Sport 3-spoke steering wheel
The truck with a Pioneer CD head unit with a detachable faceplate with SD card, USB, and AUX slots
The truck with an eBay black, weighted shift knob
The truck with its 15-inch OEM six-lug, six-spoke chrome Nissan Pathfinder rims
The truck that tucked 225 wide (fusion) tires front and back
The truck with an 18-pound Braille racing battery
The truck with Apex carbon fiber brake pads
The truck without its Blue Gates performance pulley belt
The truck with its imperfectly perfect four-color patina
The truck with its smoked corner lenses and taillights
The truck with a black bed liner
The truck with a silver pinstripe
The truck that was sold.
The truck that was a Mazda
The truck that was my Mazda.

Art by Nathaniel O. Chambers

TERRANCE D. THOMPSON

Is There a God?

Yes.
There has to be.
It's the only way to explain it:
The sun and the moon, night and day,
Seasons change, flowers bloom, animals play.
I guess they do call it nature.
Yes, I believe in the "Big Bang"—
I also believe "Let There Be" to be one and the same.
They say He lives in Heaven.
I don't know where that is,
Maybe it is in the sky.
Yeah, He must be an alien,
He's not from earth.
Could be a She. Maybe both, or neither one.
No, not like Tammy; she's different.
I'll explain that one later.
He looks like us.
The Bible says we look like them.
There must be more than one of them—
It does say "Us."
Not just our Bible, other religions too!
It could be all made up, but what
If it's not?
That's why we pray every day:
It's called Faith.
You can't see or touch air, either.
Yes, it is there.
Why is water wet?

Why is the sky blue?
Why is snow cold?
I don't know.
I guess some things just are.
He has many names.
Yes, Allah.
Yep, Jehovah, too.
And Yahweh.
Yep, Jah.
No, they're all the same.
Better to believe and be wrong
Than not to believe and be wrong.
Say your prayers.
I'll say my prayers too.
Good night,
Daddy loves you!

Three Haiku

Waves gently crashing
the song of the bait runner
my keeper striper

The rage burns within
until tonight's visit calms
the lion sleeps tonight

Her loving embrace
warms inside my soul
early morning sunrise

Ode to Nature

NETERU ...

Since the beginning of time you have reminded us of a presence divine. You are the defining proof of an existence far greater than ours. Your constants of symbiosis and duality embody all the wondrous works of He who, through one word, caused all to be. You are the morning sun, warming all that lies beneath you. You are the night moon, relaxing many worn souls through your calming glow. You are the gentle breeze, blowing soft kisses upon lovers picnicking in the field.

... OH, NETERU ...

You are the perfect example of love in a doe's protection of her fawn from wolves, the sacrifice of parental salmon as they endure the arduous journey back to their home streams. You are the lead character in the theatre of man's dreams. You are the life-giving waters of the morning dew. Even through destruction, we, mankind, have always seen the beauty in you: beautiful caves and canyons, oases in the middle of wind-blown deserts, warm pools left from violent lava flows, the vast plains swept clean by the wrath of tornadoes.

... OH, NETERU ...

You have taught us the value and efficiency of food chains where even the remotest scraps are never wasted. You are the most fragrant smells and intriguing flavors that man has ever tasted. You are the building blocks of all the wondrous constructions man has ever created. You are the endless question of "WHY?" even when our only answer is "Because it does!" You are the symphony of sounds in the jungle, the sweet silence across the arctic, the masterpiece of Aurora Borealis painted across the northern sky. You are every wonder envisioned since man first opened an eye. You are the creation, the explanation of an unseen creator that, at times, man chose to deify. You are the harmony of yin and yang, or night and day, the scales that balance life vs. decay. Because of you we have found a way . . . to search in the remotest places, to keep a smile on most of our faces. You are present in everything we see, hear, taste, smell, feel and do. Even we, also, are a part of you!

...OH, BEAUTIFUL NETERU!

RASHEEN GIRAUD

Charisma

One afternoon during the cool Indian summer, after just being stopped and frisked by the New Haven PD (which has become an all-too-customary experience for black men), I found myself at a Buffalo Wild Wings over on Church St. eating spicy chicken fingers smothered with creamy ranch dressing and sipping a thirst-quenching Coke soda, ignoring the discordant slurs and yelling of a couple of individuals that did not venerate public decency by holding a vigil outside the windows, enthralled by the race of humanity.

In that moment I was taken by the presence of an eye-pleasing, five-foot-nine, ebony-complexioned queen with her glossy, dreaded hair wrapped in a bun sitting atop her head reflecting the afternoon sunlight like a black diamond-crusted tiara. Catching my gaze, she gave me a shy but welcoming smile and, breaking eye contact, fixed the mahogany-black purse that hung fusionally from her revealed shoulder and headed into the Buffalo Wild Wings.

As I sat and watched her talk to the host, I couldn't help but reflect back to my brother's party and how she was one of the females sliding down the pole like a firefighter, and I wondered if she would remember the private dance she and I had had that night. I hoped she wouldn't, so she wouldn't feel the need to get defensive when I went to introduce myself.

As she made her way to the booth, I waited a little, to be sure she wasn't expecting company. After five minutes of technically procrastinating, I finally went to properly introduce myself.

An hour later, after dialoging about comfortable things, like school and where we were from and if we were single, neither of us had raised the question of what we did for a living. I know why I didn't inquire, but why didn't she? Though I already knew what it

156

was she did, I inquired just to get a reaction, while also hoping she did not feel judged.

She shied away from the question by changing the subject.

"There's no need to be embarrassed," I said. "I won't judge you."

"Who said I'm embarrassed?" she exclaimed with a nervous chuckle.

"No one, technically, but the truth of the matter is, people hide certain things they're ashamed of," I said with a flirtatious smirk.

She took out her phone and, as if making a text, completely disregarded everything I'd said.

"Anyway," she said with a sly smile, "what's your name again?"

"Oh, now you got jokes," I said, fixing my Cincinnati baseball fitted. "That's cool. It's Rahsheen."

"Please, Rahsheen, you act like you remember my name," she said. She gazed into my eyes and sipped her Sprite soda, then started to play with her food.

"Well, I'm sorry, Charisma, if you feel like your name is not worthy enough to be remembered. So, just because you forgot *my* name, you owe."

"I owe? What could I possibly owe *you*?" she said, as if she was aghast at what I was saying.

"Nothing wild. Just take my number and allow me to take you out one night."

She agreed by smiling from ear to ear, then she took my number and we went our separate ways.

After a few months of being platonically involved, she and I found ourselves in a more intimate relationship. Being tethered together by our attraction, we decided to make things official. In contrast to most women in her line of work, she was a very compassionate person, a peach that should be picked up and never put down. She deserved to be loved, she deserved to be saved, a vanilla-smelling, silky smooth beauty. Times are harder for women with the economy's decline, especially the ones trying to better themselves by going to school.

Paying tuition while helping keep food on the table is detrimental for anyone, let alone a female trying to live in an urban community where the odds are against the people living there. Yeah, Charisma was a stripper, and I loved her because who she was inside communicated far more elegantly than anything she said or did. Her ends justified her means.

She was a star that didn't know she shined until she eventually told me, on a white Christmas day, sitting in front of her mother's splendid, lit Christmas tree, that she wanted the world. So I saved her by making her my girl. Giving her what she deserved made me feel like our purpose was fulfilled, because we both were living life not grounded but flying in love. It was something I wanted to happen. It happened, so yeah, you could call me Captain.

A Weakness Has Revived

Before, I was weak enough to lie,
But now that I'm strong enough to tell the truth
About a weakness that revived, and strong enough to stay alive,
I've been weakened by its strength,
Then strengthened by its meaning.
My love for you is clear.
I hope it's clear that you're my weakness.

ROCKY WILLIAMS
aka THE ILLESTRATOR

Homeless Drunkard

I greet the dawn as I rise with the same ol' thoughts on my mind,
I stretch and wipe the crust from out of my eyes.
I don't remember how I got here, I couldn't surmise,
And if you ask me where I'm going, I couldn't describe.
They say every day is a new day,
It's Tuesday, I'm wondering why
It feels like I've lived this same day a hundred times.
Waking up to the front page, I dread what I've become,
But week-old news is better than none.
And so I live with regrets and the taste of last night on my breath,
After the moment's done, I'm chasing the next,
Watching life pass by me, again and again,
It started with a happy beginning but there is no end.
Thru my distorted panorama a vision of skid row,
The concrete jungle, fiends fixing to get "mo,"
Some clutching on a bag, others sucking on a glass,
'cause yesterday's failures got us stuck in the past.
We call it neverland hope 'cause we stressed and can't cope,
City streets polluted with second-hand smoke,
Worn-down shoes with a second-hand coat,
Wear a watch with the wrong time, second-hand broke,
No lions, tigers, or bears,
Just liars, buyers, and squares,
Stench of urine in the hallways, conditions of despair,
Tuesdays and Thursdays it's tension in the air,
Drug dealers spending all day pitching in the stairs,

Getting paid off mongering, competing with an honest man,
Stray dogs wandering, eating out of garbage cans,
Zombies, crazed,
Building lobbies depraved,
Narrating from the exact spot a dead body laid,
And the Feds'll probably raid but it's frivolous to mention,
Villains prey with the illest of intentions,
About mid-day they slither through the trenches,
Out back where the kids play, littered with syringes.
But the saddest thing is, I think I love it,
Crack a bottle, drink and won't stop until I reach the bottom of it.
No home, so I walk around sullenly,
The sun is out but still a dark cloud hovers me,
I'm a mad drunk, looking for a penny,
If it wasn't for bad luck, I wouldn't have any.
Sometimes it's better to lose instead of cheating,
I spent my last dollar on booze instead of eating,
I'm taunted by the folks on the ave.,
As they laugh I'm haunted by the ghosts of my past.
My dreams and ambitions never seen their fruition,
Never dreamed I'd succumb to this disease of addiction.
Daily I wind up sulking in a river,
A portrait of self-hatred, repulsive and withered.
Maybe I'll die as a result of the liquor,
Alcohol poisoning, cirrhosis of the liver,
This is the enterprise, where part of the inner dies,
Witness the genocide,
Prisoners living lies,
It's harrowing.
Pops was my hero and moms was a heroine, her veins full of heroin.
She warned me that the days'll get worse,
She said, "Prison's your second home, don't ever make it your first."

160

I bear agony's lessons, with no cares at all,
But when reality sets in, that's when the tears fall,
Then after all the weeping absorbs,
My skin reeks of alcohol, seeping through my pores,
I ain't shaved or sleek,
I ain't bathed in weeks,
I smile, though I'm ashamed of the shade of my teeth.
And the pain runs deep, so I've learned to live down bottom,
It ain't good, my neighborhood is downtrodden,
We fight and bicker and drink white liquor,
And at night the streetlights flicker, you see sights sicker.
This ain't paradise,
Life is a pair of dice.
When your number's called are you man or mice?
If you haven't trudged where I've trudged,
You don't know my pain, how can you judge?

Christmas

Christmas is my favorite holiday.
Especially a white Christmas, like this Christmas.
I can never fall asleep on Christmas Eve because I'm always so anxious
to see what I get.
The excitement of looking through presents to find which ones have
my name,
Tearing through the wrapping paper, unveiling a box,
Opening the box, unearthing gift paper,
Digging through the gift paper . . .
Long johns and socks?
(Remember to be grateful.)
Wow, just what I always wanted.

Lights line the house, inside and out.
My street looks like an arcade game.
My Christmas list was long but I don't see too many presents for me.
Some must be hidden.
Which box has the Play Station?
The smell of fresh-baked chocolate chip cookies . . . Mmm Mmm.
Christmas trees smell so good and clean,
But stepping on pine needles isn't so fun,
Nor is making sure this tree has water with sugar in it.
There isn't a fireplace in our home, but stockings are tacked to the wall.
This candy cane is helping—I wonder if they know I didn't brush.
For me, Mommy? Thank you!
Stetson cologne, soap, and deodorant?
Just what I always wanted.

At least if there was a Santa Claus, I could be upset with him for this
boring Christmas.

Oh, new boots, a new coat! Thanks . . .
Just what I always wanted.

I usually look forward to my cousins coming over so we can talk
about what we got.
Not this year though.
No video game, no boom box, no toys, no fun.
I just want to go back to sleep.

I can't wait till *next* Christmas.

Yesterday, Today, Tomorrow

Yesterday was a good day,
Today was better.
Tomorrow's a day I'll remember forever.
September 3, 2009,
We exchanged vows, she was all mine.
A check on my wish list,
Justice of the Peace and one witness,
Sunny, green grass of the summer—
The moment seems endless.

Yesterday was a good day,
Today was better.
Tomorrow's a day I'll remember forever.
Holding hands as we exchange glances,
Trying to remain calm while my soul dances.
I married the woman I love . . .
I'm happy, and I should be
Thinking of our future, and how things could be.

Yesterday was a good day,
Today was better.
Tomorrow's a day I'll remember forever.
If the future doesn't look as good as the now or before,
Is it worth the heartache that you're bound to endure?
I can't answer for you,
I can only just try.
But if it's not worth it in the end,
I'll enjoy the ride.

CHARLES DEVORCE

Vivian, Auntie

You were the one, out of all the aunts, when it came to being babysat, all the children in the family cried out, "Please, Mom, can we stay with Aunt So-and-so? Please, Mom, *she's* too strict! We always have to clean up after we eat or do the yard. Sometimes we can't even *leave* the yard. And if she's busy in the house we can't even go off the porch. None of us—your four, her two. Little-ass porch!"

As I got older, able to reflect and contemplate, I saw what a monumental task it was operating a Chinese laundry out-of-house, preparing dinner—even snacks at times—all while maintaining safe vigilance over six energetic kids. Respect you for that! And that day after school, you read my first poem, though I had no idea what a poem was, and I heard you tell my mother, "Girl, this boy can write. For his age, his words come together nice." You never had a clue, but at that moment you inspired me. And though the fire only smolders of late, it is still lit. And, too, because of your loving admiration, your words overheard, you, in my heart, went from being Aunt Meanie to the one who made sure we kids were provided for and safe. From being just "Vivian, Auntie," to being, out of all the aunts, my favorite, "Auntie Vivian"!

Love you.

R & B Legend Marvin Gaye Shot Dead By Father

At first my brain rejected what my eyes had relayed to it. That lasted but a nano-second, until the lady, quite visibly distraught, came running out of a salon yelling, "Oh my God! Oh my God! They killed him!" Obviously, she hadn't realized that "they" was his own father. I'll never forget it. I was living in Kansas at the time, and to say I was in shock would be to downplay everything I was beginning to feel. Wow. Marvin Gaye. Damn. Marvin the Marvelous, master crooner, King of R & B, owner of late night love sessions—dead at forty-four years old.

Never forget, Marv, how you boosted my courage up to step to the ladies After the Dance, or how my boldness was reinforced after hearing the hit "I Want You"—which, I might add, led to many nights and days of Sexual Healing. And especially how a Distant Lover became my wife.

April 1, 1984. Huh . . . April Fool's Day. If only this tragedy could've been a prank. But it was real—you were gone. Consumed beyond repair by demons, and then finally gone. Yet in my mind, my memory, and my heart you live on. Had no idea that your smash hit "Trouble Man" (one of my all-time favorites) was *you*, a very troubled man. Miss you, and may your soul be at peace, and music of your soul, truly soul music, sing on.

Damn. Marvin!

ALEXIS "LEX" MELENDEZ

Just Like Me (A Monologue)

Here's my pass and I.D. I know the routine.

"Melendez, visit."

Damn, he looks just like me . . . Walks just like me . . . Talks just like me . . . Now he's telling me he wants to *be* just like me? It breaks my heart.

So you want to be just like me? But I turned out to be nothing like I wanted to be. You think I want to see you wear these tans, just like me? Taking those trips, risking your life, just like me. I haven't held you since you were three—you're thirteen! The price I thought I paid so you would turn out nothing like me!

Hold up, let me finish.

Where was I? Oh, yeah. So you think you could win at a game that plays for keeps, just like me? You think you got a bullet-proof plan, just like me? You think that money will save the fam, just like me? Just 'cause you made it home from running from the police last night, you think you made it home scot-free, just like me?

Listen, Lex Junior, as much as I love you, I love me too. But you should never want to be just like me! If anything, aspire to be what I *wanted* to be . . . like a lawyer, a doctor, or even your own dream!

You still think the risk is worth the reward, just like me? You think two years of balling is worth losing your late 20s, all of your 30s, and nine of your 40s, just like me? You think you'll enjoy watching your kids grow old from behind this glass at only one hour a week, just like me? Or spending Thanksgiving, Christmas, and birthdays with the fam through a Kodak moment, just like me?

Being told over the phone that your dad got hit by a drunk driver and didn't make it; told over that same phone that your mom got dementia and won't even know you when you come home, just like me?

So, do you still want to be just like me?

Oh. I didn't know . . . I thought you were talking about who I *was*, not who I *became*. I'm sorry for going in on you before you finished what you were saying.

So when you have a kid you're going to be a great father . . . just like me!

Paper Thin

Whoever said money can't buy happiness must not have been able to afford it! Because my happiest days were when I was rich. Now I lost the best years of my life chasing you without looking at the price tag until it was too late—because the price turned out to be the best years of my life to everyone I ever loved, from my mom to my grandpa, to girls, to my own kids ... If I had never gone for broke, I would never have known the love people had for me was paper thin.

Money, you don't make me, I made you, and was willing to die before I let anyone take you from me. Yeah, yeah, I took a few losses, but I made you back before daybreak, and caught you sleeping with 30,000 of your closest friends! I protected you with my life, hid you everywhere from my mattress to a fireproof safe three feet deep.

When your creator started printing big faces I held onto the old heads as if spending one of you would have been disloyal, because once you reached your maker it was the end of your journey—no more putting food on the family's table; diamonds on my girl's fingers, ears, and neck; clothes on my back; and smiles on faces.

Chasing a quicker get-rich scheme led us straight to Foxwoods and Mohegan Sun. Those days I had to drive home after losing you was the worst—ask Tracy, Tawnesha, or Jahanna! The ride back was spent on the Nextel trying to get paid by the dozen who took work on consignment. Damn, they had excuses when it came to coming off you. But how could I blame them when a pocketful of you meant the sky was the limit? Never once was I alone when I had you. Never once was a pretty face not by my side, never once was I not able to fix a frown or a problem with a handful of you, and never once when I had you did I see the true colors of those around me ... Damn, you made me blind.

I don't know whom I hate more, them or you. Then again, how could I blame you when I made you? So, I guess I hate me for giving you and them my all.

The sad thing is, we are destined to meet again. But this time, no risk will be taken, no fast money will be made. If it ain't worth working for, it ain't worth having. If the outcome even has a chance of being a loss, I ain't playing!

Don't get me wrong. The game was fun, payday was good, and my life was great. But the price I'm paying cost me my life, and for what? Fast money, faster cars, and the fastest chicks!

Well, money, this is it. No more playing your fool. No more quick flips. No more ski mask money. This is it, I'm going to make it without the fast version of you, you'll see! And my kids will never know about that life because I'm teaching them that there is more to life than money—so you won't catch no wins with none of mine!

So, money, thanks for everything, but no thanks. I'll earn mine without risk. I'm done risking my life for you. So if you ever find yourself in my pocket, it will only come from getting change or cashing checks at the bank!

Sincerely,
Your Biggest Fan

A Letter

Dear Judge,

I really don't know why my daddy doesn't walk me to the school bus anymore, or doesn't tuck me in at night, or why I can only see him for an hour a week through a window—the same windows they have at the zoo. I really don't know why.

At night, when I pretend to be sleeping, I can hear my mommy cry and pray to God that the judge will let my daddy come home soon. And when Grammie comes over I hear her tell Mommy things about my daddy, and when they notice me playing with my Tonka truck they start to spell out their words so I can't understand. And when my daddy calls, I have to press "1"—I found that out after I pressed the wrong number and Daddy couldn't call for three days.

The reason I'm writing to you is because I hear that your job is to play God and judge those who stand before you, and my daddy is coming before you on January 15. The reason I know is because I got a play at school that day and Mommy can't make it because Daddy got court. From what I hear, my daddy has to come before you for trying to feed his kids and keeping clothes on our backs. So I sat Alicia down (she's my little sister) and I told her she can't have Daddy buy her everything she sees that is pink, and I won't ask for every new pair of Jordans that comes out—but I need one more pair—and we will only eat one snack a day so the food will last. So, since I came up with a solution, problem solved!

So, Judge, will you send my daddy home now?

Sincerely yours,

Lex, Jr.

P.S. I don't really need the Jordans.

Untitled

Life . . . the only thing we truly get one of. So let me give you directions to the road less traveled, so you don't fall victim to the I-95 to nowhere.

This is how you wake up for school on time.
This is how you graduate on time.
This is how you apply to college.
This is how you avoid my mistakes!

See, when it's all said and done, it all comes down to the choices we make when no one is looking. Write it, regret it, say it, forget it. So put that smart phone down and pick up what *I'm* putting down.

Always look a person in the eyes.
Never tell a lie you can't make come true.
Always hold your head up high.
Never let them see you sweat.
Always stand up for the underdog.
Never back down.
Always hold yourself to the highest standard.
Never settle for less.
Always speak up . . .
But never miss the opportunity to shut up.
Revenge imprisons us, but forgiveness sets us free.
You will be rich if you're satisfied with what you have.
One is truly wise who gains his wisdom from the experience of others.
And you may give without loving, but you can't love without giving, so be ready to give and be willing to share, and sometimes when you forget the gift, you disrespect the giver.

See, Nas, these jewels I'm dropping on you took me a lifetime to collect. Some were given to me for a small fee, while others took me years to learn through trials and tribulations. And I'm giving them to you for the low-low.

Life comes with no remote. Now get up and change the channel!

I Remember

Dear Mom, I miss you, living life without you is an issue.
Beat, bruised, battered, heart is shattered.
Dementia took your mind while the state took my time!
I remember when it started—a year ago to the day
When you forgot it was my birthday.
No calls, no letters, no cards were sent,
The day came and went.
So I reached out to my brother through Securus,
He pressed "1" and the words came through the phone
And snatched my breath and my soul:
"Mom got dementia and didn't remember!"
The thought still leaves tears on my pillow!

Dear Mom, I miss you, living life without you is an issue.
Beat, bruised, battered, heart is shattered.
I hold onto our memories because if I let go
They're gone forever
And if I were ever granted a wish
It would be to give Mom back her memory!
We used to laugh, now that noise is hardly heard.
You used to say my name in every prayer,
Now you only ask me what my name *is*!

Dear Mom, I miss you, living life without you is an issue.
Beat, bruised, battered, heart is shattered.
You look the same, yet you don't remember my face.
The pain of the reality of losing my mom
Without losing my mom brought me to losing my heart
Without losing my heart.
When you're sitting in front of me
All I do is hope you remember me!

The Gift and the Curse

I can remember my first memory of my father. I can remember wishing one of these birthday wishes would come true. It was September 4th, 1989, and I was turning five, and without even thinking he gave me a gift that some parents wish they could buy on a shelf in a store. You see, I've seen the campaign *Say No to Drugs*—the egg in the pan, "This is your brain on drugs"—but that was just an egg in a pan. My dad was lying with a needle in his hand, no beat in his heart, piss in his pants. Smelled like death from the start. But I saved his life that day—a simple call, help was on the way. We became close after that day, but no balls were thrown, no fish were caught, no fatherly stuff. Defined by a choice—like I even had a choice!—been gone so long my son got a son and my daughter never seen me out of tans! I've been depressed and oppressed, dehumanized and ostracized. You see, Dad, I was raised seeing so much wrong that I thought it was right.

At eleven I was handed a mask and a note, told to walk to the teller, get the money, and run!

Now, Dad, what do you call that?

Cashing a check, son. Now don't tell your mother!

At twelve I was my dad's apprentice at the local Spot-n-Steal, some more wrongs that seemed so right. Caught my first case, they claimed grand theft but I swore it was just a "joy ride."

Thirteen spent in detention, long lane, and residentials.

Fourteen, I'm freed. Dad's still on the scheme but strung like no guitar I ever seen, so I was on my own, never had a plan, just putting pieces together from hindsight. Two wrong turns followed by a million right never did get me back to ground zero!

Fifteen/sixteen, I'm on the varsity team, grades so good Mrs. Olson swore I was cheating. I was only cleared after all three kids around me failed. I never did get an apology, or better yet another ace—and it's not that I couldn't. I would just leave the last four blank, just enough to get a passing grade.

Sixteen, I signed up to be all you can be, like you see in the commercials on TV. Figured I'd make the family proud. My first right choice that seemed so right, but in my dad's eyes it was oh so wrong!

Needless to say, at seventeen I stood in front of the judge and was given five years a month before graduation, so instead of receiving my diploma and heading off to college, I was stamped a felon and sent off to Yale—I mean *jail*. Now my options of a career are slim to none.

Eighteen, I earned my GED at MYI, was even the motivational speaker, made the town of Cheshire front page—even ended with "This one's for you, Mom!"

Nineteen, lying on my bunk, watching the news, I found out my dad was killed. Just a week earlier we'd had our last words over him hitting my mother. I told him, "I wish you would die," then I blew out my candles. Who would have thought that wish I made when I was five would one day come true? The gift and the curse!

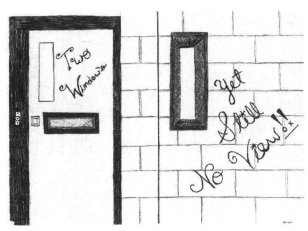

Drawing by Alexis Melendez

Still Life with a Door, Two Windows, and Three Walls

A steel door weighing
As much as all the doors in your house would weigh,
Protecting in value what you would put on the curb
With a "Free" sign on it. With the exception of family photos
Which we hold dear, sort of like the family heirlooms
You keep locked in a safe.
Two windows, yet still no view,
Just like I wrote my last line without my "eyes."
No, for real, without the letter "I"!
Three walls that sweat in the summer
And freeze in the winter like something left outside,
Like that bum you step by on your way to get high.
They claim to be painted white, but white is bright,
So that ain't right. It's more like the color of depression
With a splash of hate, as if hate and depression had
A color! But hey, welcome to Cell A-123.

Play Ball

I was born with one strike:
Mom was on welfare.
Realized years later I started out with two:
Dad was a fiend, addicted to the lean.
So it was no surprise to be struck out when I was just a teen,
Had to play the bench,
Await my next at-bat.
They claimed it would take 18,
But I was back at-bat in the 6th,
Somehow I managed to earn a walk!
On the next pitch they missed the mark,
So I stole second.
I weighed so much on the pitcher's mind,
He balked, and the judge granted me third.
But now I'm stuck,
So I call my DH.
Like, "Grandpa, please call Barry Bonds,
Tell him I'm trying to see the post."
Before I knew it, I was walking out.
Lesson learned.
I'm home!

From Point "A" to Point "B"

You entered my life at a time when God knew someone like you wouldn't do, and that I needed exactly you. My prayer is that when you read this you won't take it as me talking down to you and can understand that I only wrote this as a reminder to yourself of your true value . . . Because to the world you may be only one person, but to Grandpa and me, you are the world.

Now I know you go above and beyond for the both of us without looking at the price tag or thinking twice, but the route you're taking might take our world away, leaving us floating in space like some abandoned satellite's debris. And I know we mean more to you than that, and losing us would be like losing the ability to smile, because when you go days on end without seeing us, you go just as long without a smile.

So, you need to see that you're traveling in a direction with no direction . . . You just go from point "A" to cross your fingers and pray that you make it through the day without obtaining some new cuffs! And your longevity is a little shorter than the long arms of the law, so you need to see that those night classes are a lot better than a night in a cell.

So, I guess what I'm trying to say is, take a risk on yourself, invest in your future, and uncross your fingers, because we'll get to point "B" together.

Untitled

Lately, sleep has been hard to come by,
and mornings have been the worst.
Every day I open my eyes a part of me dies.
Staring into these dirty white walls
that you know are clean, yet they're not!
Walls that have the power to turn
the biggest heart into the Grinch!
Can you believe
life has come to this?

Now each day I count the days
despite a wise man telling me,
Don't date the days cause a date don't change the day
and flipping the page don't change the page—all that
does is change the page,
sort of like *Groundhog Day*.
But nobody remembers me anymore!

And then one day my family
shows up for a visit . . . It's been four years
since my last one . . . My son walks in
and with one word he gives me life . . .

Dad!

Untitled

If you can cross all your T's and dot all your I's,
then write away your life story without using one "if."
If you can blindly trust your closest friend with your darkest secret
knowing that one day it will come to light, then whisper away.
If you can love and not be tired by loving
or being used, then don't deal in used ones;
. . . or being cheated, then don't give way to cheating;
and never make the next one pay for the last one.

If you can deal with hearing your grandfather's dying wish to
see you a free man, knowing he won't, then take that wrong turn.
If you can deal with dreaming about days you've already lived over
and over
because you threw your future away, then take that risk.
If you can meet with guilty and not guilty
and treat the two just the same, then suit up and wait your turn.

Son, the middle of my l-**if**-e was what it was because of those ifs.
You're still young enough to enjoy the word "if,"
but if it was up to me, you would be everything I wasn't.
If I was you, I would hate me . . .
If I was you, I would hate me . . .
If I was you, I would hate me . . .
Wait. You're not me, because your heart is full of love for me, your dad.
Thanks.

KENNETH ANDERSON

A Letter

Dear Mr. Warden,

My name is Kinani and I am five but I'm gonna be six next year when I go to the kindergarten school and the bus brings me. Ummm, I was thinking, is my Pa Pa Kenny over there? Because I need my hair cut for school. I saw him on the TV. Do you have his helicopter plane over there? He said he was gonna take me and Kinora to the beach and fly his helicopter plane. You like rollercoasters? Pa Pa Kenny made me laugh. Grandma said she's gonna let me talk to Pa Pa Kenny when he calls from his truck. Did you ride in Pa Pa Kenny's big, big truck? OMG! It's bigger than a spaceship! But I have to go now. Tell my Pa Pa Kenny to come home now because I need my hair cut for school next year. Oh—and tell him don't forget to bring the helicopter plane.

Father Monologue

Ya Ya, this is the fourth suspension this month, and I'm not gonna take off another day of work because you won't do right. This BS stops right here and now! Ya know, what you really need is for me to break you off a little something because I really don't think you're hearing me, and I'm to the point where I feel the need to reach out and touch you with this strap. Boy, you have no idea how good you've got it, and then I think you do know and this is why you're out there at school acting up. Ya know, I've sat down and had a heart to heart talk with you before in regards to your attitude and its negative effects. I warned you of this very incident. You think that acting out in school is gonna make your father come by or run to your aid. Now listen, you're going about it the wrong way. The only one who's getting hurt is you. Hey, I know you love your father and you want him in your life. Trust me, I get that, but going out there and being disrespectful to your teachers is not going to make him come by. I've called him, your mother's called him, so he is aware of the situation and has been from day one. He has yet to return any of my calls. But even all that still does not warrant your behavior in school. It's so embarrassing when I have to go and look in the face of your administrators every other month about the same things. It really makes me feel incompetent as a parent and my position in this family. And God knows I've been there for you. If you don't get your priorities right—and quick!—you're gonna end up a statistic, and nobody is gonna want to be around you. All your so-called friends will go on to their other grades and you're gonna be left behind. You're lucky they haven't expelled you because of your discipline issues. Your mom and I work so hard to make sure you and your brother and sister have what you need, and this is how you say thank you? So let me tell you what's gonna happen now. I'm going old school on you. You no longer have a free ticket in this house. Your needs will be met. Your clothing you already have—nothing new; the sneakers—nothing new. You will be fed. However, your liberty belongs to me. All your wants are gonna cost you daily. I know all this I'm imposing on you you're not gonna like, but you gotta understand I'm trying to save you from where you're headed.

Where I'm From

I'm from a place no small kids wanted to be.
Hi. My name?
Um . . . I don't know.
Balloon in one hand, my baby brothers in the other.
Scary for me. Who are these people?

A place where the mother was always there
And the father didn't really care.
Well . . . about *us*. The newcomers.

A place where the food was plentiful:
In the cupboards and freezers and refridge . . .
OMG! All these sweets, cookies, and cakes,
Jellybeans and red-hot dollars!
(Hand in the bowl) *Slap!!!*
"You don't touch nothing in this house,
Understand?"
Tears fell because I was hurt and I didn't understand why
I had to work so hard.
I'm only five and I'm tired.
I'm hungry and I want to go home.
Oh, I forgot—this *is* home.

A place where feet were on the floor
At six every morning, but it's not a school day.
Can't I sleep?
"No! And that bed better be made."

A place where my playground . . . Oops,
I forgot. Didn't have one of those.

"Better be in sight when I look out the window, boy!"

 Can I go to the corner store, ma?
"No! Ain't got no money,
 you ain't got no job,
 what you going to the store for?
 Man don't work, he'll steal.
 Money don't grow on trees."

A place where you got one suit, three pair of pants,
 Six undershirts and bottoms, six socks,
 Two pair of sneakers (skippies, they called them),
 And one pair of shiny, big, pilgrim-buckle, black dress shoes
 (well, my oldest brother passed them down to me).
 I sho' would like a pair of them Pro Keds.
"No!"

A place where nothin' was given.
 Wow! Nothing?
 A place where high expectations was demanded,
 Failure not an option, education forever.
"Boy, go get me that encyclopedia."

But ma, I've memorized my world and state capitals,
 My Roman numerals, multiplication tables, the presidents.
 Yes, I know my social security number.
 I've cleaned my room, the bathroom,
 I've vacuumed the carpet, cleaned the windows,
 Washed the dishes, scrubbed the floor.
 My knees hurt.
 Can I go out and play?
"Come here and scratch my head."

A place where fish was every Friday
And spaghetti was on Saturday. Ummmm ...
Where mine's at?
"Boy, eat them leftovers and be glad you eatin' at all.
Don't look at me like that."

A place where being left in the hot car all day was the norm,
Especially for school shopping and groceries.
Where was the police man then?
Hot and hungry for what seemed to be an eternity.
(Knock, knock, knock. Excuse me, Mr. White Man,
but can I have some of your ice cream?
What?)

A place where being hungry stirred the curiosity
Of eating niblets from Brandy's—
The neighbor's border collie's—
Dish.
(Hey boy, come here. Can I have some?
Ruff!)

A place where how your day was didn't matter
And nobody knew, and you better not complain.
That basement was dark and cold,
Tied up in that blanket on that concrete floor all night.
Felt like the morgue.

A place where mere words, or certain looks,
Would have your mouth on fire,
Cayenne pepper, ninety degrees in the sun, dyin' of thirst.
"Go sit on that stoop and you better not move!

Water's for cowards."

A place where winters were cold
But not as cold as the lack of affection we had to endure.
"Affection?
Man up, boy! This ain't no world for sissies."

Graduation Day.
Can I get a hug? A kiss? A "Well done"?
Or "Proud of you, boy. Good job. Thank you"?
Hmm, how about this one: "Son, I love you"?

No.

JAMAR BOYD

Pyro

When I was nine years old, I had a fascination with fire. I would grab lighters left unattended around the house and go outside and grab a pile of leaves, light them on fire, and run. My fascination with starting fires increased as I noticed my friends BJ and Fat Mike being so scared they would run, only to find me later on and tell me how cool it was to see the fire start off so small then get so big it would illuminate the whole side of the building. I was immediately taken by their fear and excitement and felt a need to take it to another level. I then came up with another experiment which I knew would add to the fear and excitement of my peers, as well as my own. I found out through my experiments that when I lit an empty water bottle on fire it would drip hot fire droplets and make a noise that I can only describe as when I play my MegaMan video game and the sound that comes on when I shoot his plasma gun. So, as this noise echoed while fire droplets fell to the ground, I decided to let it drip on a few lighters in an attempt to blow them up. I stood back, not knowing exactly what would happen, and after a few minutes it was like the best fireworks I'd ever seen on the Fourth of July. There was a loud BANG that resembled the sound at night when the thugs in the neighborhood would shoot at each other with their pistols over drugs or to protect their turf. Then it was followed by a bright orange and red fireball, which lit up like a miniature sun that came to life and brightened everything in sight with light speed timing. Me and BJ ran for dear life down the street while Fat Mike struggled to keep up. A police officer on a bicycle heard the loud bang and seen us three kids running from a backyard. He was only able to catch Fat Mike due to his fatigue. The officer brung Mike down to the police station and during the interrogation Mike immediately gave me up, along with my whereabouts. Police officers showed up to my house and arrested me for fire starting and breach of the peace. I was sent to a juvenile detention center.

Wake Up, Chinx

I was in my prison cell listening to my favorite radio station, Hot 93.7, when breaking news interrupted one of my all-time favorite songs. DJ Big Man seemed very upset as he apologized for cutting off the song and proceeded to explain the need for the interruption: "Chinx died Saturday morning at three a.m." He explained that Chinx had been shot while driving in his vehicle. I instantly felt disturbed, as the beginning of a bad day had begun. I dropped my radio onto my bed and placed one of my mix tapes—the Coke Boys—into my CD player to reminisce on the numerous TV and radio interviews that I'd heard of Chinx. It was another sad day in the hip hop community, and we all had to be careful of how we did our daily activities, being mindful of our loved ones and that tomorrow isn't promised. Chinx was a good man who loved his family and gave his all to his community. Perhaps the same community that was instrumental in his death—so say the rumors. His cool, calm, collected style and slick-talk lyrics will always be recited during times of remembrance in school cafeterias and radio stations across the nation. Chinx, may you rest in peace, and you will never be forgotten.

CHAUNCEY WATTS

Where I'm From

I'm from a place where the clouds are dark, half-smiles and poverty
shows its face
Warm nights with the flash of lights, drug abuse controls the pace
Where bright minds fall victim to the illusion who only just wants
a taste
Young women with children become objects of narcissistic mind state
Where men become boys and fathers become children and children
become the beginning of a
cycle that will never end

I'm from a place where the sun is bright, whole smiles and positive
energy controls the pace
Where negativity never wins and faith becomes the friend
The thought of honesty becomes a mirror that no one wants to face
I'm from a place where I'm not from
I'm from a place where it just begun
I'm from a place where I control the pace
Where are you from?

A Beautiful Day

It's a beautiful day.
It's a beautiful day.
You have a choice to feel this way.
Smile and embrace what productivity has to offer.
Open your eyes, look a little deeper and wonder
Why all the laughter.
He didn't make it,
She didn't make it,
Take a deep breath,
Ahh ... we made it.
Atonement along with accountability,
Second chance versus no responsibility.
A genius with the ability to learn.
It's a beautiful day.
Your emotions confirm this day.
Blue skies mixed with the sound of splashing water,
Sunshine warms your skin,
The sweet taste of only your favorite.
Relax, disregard your fears.
Here come the men who made it in the eyes of inner success.
It's a beautiful day.

Champion Horse

I'm running faster and faster. The leather strap hits my back. The metal grinds my teeth. The pain, the frustration. I should stop now, but I'm a winner, a fighter. I will win this race. I was created to help, to pull, to carry, to assist the weak. My body and mind are built for this. They're using me for financial recognition, public praise. I'm so beautiful, my skin glows in the sun, shines in the night. I'm almost mystical. The stages in my life: from the most adorable (children love me); a stallion becomes me. The world needs me. Those who envy compete, but we're all in the same race. The finish line is a line that will never be crossed. Jump on my back. I will help you get across.

Please Turn Off the Radio

Oh, so young but oh so talented. Poetry mixed with pain and his struggle. Influenced by the sweet sound of Miles Davis but transcendent into an aggressive poetic flow. A contrast from love music. No baby making, only words depicting events when a life is taken. The bass is booming while the treble is low. More rhythm than blues as the chorus sings "Dear Mama."

Who could have thought 25-year-old Shakur could be a victim of the allure of bright lights, acts of violence, a statistic of never seeing another day? The sound that penetrates the young and breathe the words grandmothers say crazy talk, or words that only reflect something so dark. This can't be in a human being's heart. But it's only music. Their music, our world, to the opposite of I love you. 2Pac's pain, but it becomes everyone's struggle.

Please turn off the radio.

But He is Homeless

For a moment there I thought life couldn't get any better.
Some say his life couldn't be any worse.
Surrounded by the stench,
Smell liquor while stepping over puddles of piss.
Who could have thought having so little would mean so much
To a man who feels he had enough?
No car, no garage, just a house.
Home is wherever you lay your head at,
The park bench or a sleeping mat.
No liberties in that cage full of rage and madness.
They will never feel the rain
Or embrace a day absent of the sadness.
How ironic it could be,
A homeless bum in the street is actually living better than me,
The prisoner.

The Choice I Own

I own the freedom of choice. The freedom to make a better decision even when I have no choice. This liberty has been with us from day one. A choice to choose integrity and become the odd one. A choice to refuse to be reduced to a moment. A choice to chase after a dream and reach for the stars and grab it like I own it. A choice to challenge stereotypes. A choice to make things right. A choice to go beyond all expectations. A choice to own a choice. This solution to understand there is a choice to oppress. A choice to treat others in a manner that highlights our best. A choice to say I'm ready for the challenges of what's next. A choice to fight until there is nothing left.

Education is the Key

How powerful are the words which rang loud like a cry for help on a rooftop. Silence as the evasive boom travels to the ear drum. Words without wisdom cut deep into the heart of those seeking answers, but there are no questions. Aimlessly following the herd. And wonder if this is life's purpose. Can a TV screen provide everything we need? Or are the masses lazier than a bum whose hardships came because he refused to read? Tangible salvation floats in the sky like words from the scriptures. Think independently or one day you will say, "Damn, how did life's beautiful kiss miss me?"

The Opposite of Paradise

As I awaken from last night's dreams of paradise, I realize my dreams are a reality that I could now see. Prison walls of concrete and metal, prison recreation so loud one would think someone is playing heavy metal. But it is only a card game, a game where losers feel like the winner, a game where a sinner travels a road full of pain and despair, touching the hearts of those who are afraid to exhibit fear while tasting hope mixed with the aroma of last night's prison meal. These thoughts are a fantasy to a world of someone's last reality. Thank God there are good people who work here. As I close my eyes I awaken to the truth of a paradise. No prison walls and just a reprieve season, with atonement. Success comes to those who really want to own it. Nothing is free, 2027 a journey to my final reality.

Silent Words

I want my words to challenge everything you thought was right.

I want my words to make you think on a higher plane and wonder how can one word bring so much pain or heal a broken heart but at the same time change a nation.

I want my words to make you smile, captivate your heart but at the same time ensure our love never grows apart.

I want my words to take you to a place where your heart is afraid to embrace, bring you to the horizon of peace, surrounded by love, change your perspective, bring out the greater you.

I want my words to motivate you to hope in a better day and wish that Trump wasn't here to stay.

I want my words to challenge your inner thoughts and make you uncomfortable.

But never forget that there is someone greater who actually loves you.

The One Who Refuses to Listen

I'm fifteen years old, I know everything. Can't nobody tell me nothing. Listen to my parents, for what? When I'm sad and blue, I keep my feelings to myself. Talk to my schoolteacher, for what? The counselor can't help me. They don't understand me. I'm fifteen years old and they are living a life like old people. My friends are all I got. So what, they smoke that stuff? I'm doing my own thing. I know what I'm doing. "Boom!" The echo's in the air from a sound that could be a gunshot.

Late at night, I hang past my curfew. Momma's words hit me like a basketball after school in the gymnasium. Moments like this, I wish I had a friend. I wish I would have listened. I wish Grandma's words would have been the truth that I have accepted. But I refuse. I open my eyes and realize the loud boom is just an old dump truck. I'm fifteen years old, can't nobody tell me nothing. But I think it is time to start listening to someone, because I'm fifteen years old and I really don't know nothing.

D. PASCHAL, *aka* K. L. PASCHAL-BARROS

Patience

I do not give you enough of my time. You're good to know and a sure way to help me grow. I spend more time with my acquaintances Anxiety and Desperation. But you are true. If only there were times I would be more like you and your brother Success, I could learn a lot. But mostly I chill with Regret and Laziness. Though when I do have you around you bring our good friends Wisdom and Happiness. So maybe we can work something out and I can have you around more often. Thank you, my friend Patience.

Where I Am From

A place where projectiles of prejudice spread quicker than the black plague in a quarantined room with people who have physical open wounds, not to count emotional ones. A place once known to have a dog as man's best friend but now it's the IBMs or the stack of Franklins. Where the best way to survive sometimes is to not be born. The land where the quickest way to the top is the fastest descent to the infinite floor of rock bottom. Where a mother's Tears in the spring are not caused by the fresh pollen but from the roots of the haunting memories of her ten-year-old son killed by a few drive-by bullets he received instead of a high school diploma. The idea of Pangaea is as true as Satan passing a polygraph. This is where I'm from, and no matter what piece of land you may be on, if you look around, so is everyone else. Welcome to Planet Earth.

LAWRENCE PERRY

Father to Son

Don't worry, son, it's just me, Mom's still outside with the rest of
the crowd.
I tried to get her to come in with me, but she said somethin' about
the silence just being too LOUD.
I don't know . . .

But she did want me to tell you that she loves you, and she really hopes
you're not mad, but you know how she is with goodbyes.
Truthfully, she just doesn't want you leavin' with the last thought in
your mind being of your mother with tears in her eyes.

As for me, I don't know what hurts me more, seeing you go or seeing
you stay, Because, son, you have a problem, and no matter how hard
we pray, or how long we delay, it's clear that this problem just won't
go away.

Son, this is so painful to say, but I have to send you away,
Because you're the best thing in my life, but seeing you like this has
truly become the worst part of my day.

Mom says it's my fault, that this is just God cursin' you because of
my life of sin,
And how you won't give up fighting because I taught you to never be
a quitter, but, SON, this here is a battle we just can't win.
I know you HATE hearing this—if it were up to you, you'd fight
until the last bell has wrung—
But enough is enough, I throw in the towel, son, as your father I just
need to do what needs to be done.

Wow, that was strange to hear, huh? Because a FATHER is somethin'
I haven't been to you—NOPE, not in some years.

And I'm so sincere when I say I apologize, because I know if I was
there, you wouldn't be here.
And I REGRET it! Damn, son, there it goes, I said it.
When the streets came to take you, I should've never stood by . . .
and let it.

But today we'll fix your problem, we'll end it and give it a fresh start
And no matter how far apart we are you'll always remain the closest
thing to my heart.

So when you get to where you're going and get settled into your
new home
Promise me you'll come back, if not for me, for Mom, just to keep
her company when she's alone.
Protect her, comfort her when the tears fall down her face
And when the cold, dark nights come, shine your light and give her
the warmest embrace.

All right, it's time, son, let's solve your problem. Just know my mind,
body, and soul are all full of love
As I say these last words:
I LOVE YOU, SON!

All right, doctor, I'm ready. Pull the plug.

I Will Not

I will not be my father!
I will not get caught in my own tangled web weaved with lies and deceit.
I will not plant my feet in this quicksand commonly called the streets.
I will not follow someone else's truth, a misconceived doctrine.
I will not make people a priority when they only make me an option.
I will not love when it's easy, then leave when it's hard.
I will fight to defend love, I will bleed, I will scar.

I will not be my father!
I will not choose personal wants over family needs.
I will not destroy my seeds by watering weeds.
I will not have my kids grow up thinking they're destined to fail.
I will not reward loyalty with even the thought of betrayal.
I will not love those who harm me, and harm those who love me.
I will keep God and Family always above me.

I will not be my father!
I will not take more than I ever plan to give.
I will not just be alive, but I will actually live.
I will be an angel to all and a devil to none.
I will shoot kind words from my mouth and not bullets from guns.
I won't bang for a gang, not for a chain with my name
That I'll get robbed for on the same corners that I hang.
I will not force myself to have heaven on earth just because I know
I'm destined for hell.
I will not go to jail and raise my children from a cell.

I will not be my father! I refuse to be anything like that man.

I will not be my father! But it's too late, kuz I think I already am.

Where I'm From

I'm from HIS greatest mistake that could've been avoided with protection.

I'm from HER brilliant plan, executed to perfection.

I'm from that drug king's nightmare; I'm from this black queen's dream.

I'm from a wise young dope dealer falling victim to an old crack fiend's scheme.

I'm from HIS temptation with fornication and lack of consideration for penetration and raw ejaculation.

I'm from HIS lack of sexual education.

I'm from HER preparation, HER precise calculation of the act of persuasion through the use of flirtation.

I'm from HER initiation of a conversation that was a combination of mind and body stimulation.

I'm from HER sexual manipulation.

I'm from HIS lows, which then became HER highs.

I'm from where nine months of those highs almost led to my demise.

I'm from a premature birth, where I was almost GONE before I ever even arrived.

I'm from where doctors replaced "Congratulations, it's a boy" with "Congratulations . . . it's alive."

I'm from where the truth hurt so much, growing up I actually found comfort in the lies.

I'm from where there's no fear in being bad, because early on you learn that even when you're good

Santa still never visits.

I'm from two parents who gave me life but neither ever taught me how to live it.

I'm from where you live your nightmares and watch as everyone else's dreams shatter.

But who cares, because the question is not where I'm from but where I'm going that matters.

The Proposal

Will you marry me?
If you promise to cherish me, I'll promise to cherish you too.
Let's not wait to set the date, kuz even soon is too late,
And I wanna show you thanks, for you were the one who carried
me through.
When that storm overtook me, when it felt like God overlooked me,
All those years living life without money, when that judge gave
me twenty,
When I thought that I was finished, when my spirit was diminished,
When I couldn't bear the burden, you kept me focused and determined,
You took the weight off my shoulders
And taught me that, as long as I have you, nothing is ever really over.
Sometimes I really hate how much I love you,
Other times I would love to say I hate you,
Because when my life is in a mess and I'm under a lot of stress,
Sometimes you'll turn off your GPS and make it hard to locate you,
And even though it was painful I don't want to sound ungrateful,
Because really I am thankful,
Because when I was stuck in the rain, when my mind, body, and soul
were drained,
You're the person to blame why I lived to SEE the rainbow.
They say you never know how good you got something until it's gone,
And when you left, they said I would be all right, but they were wrong.
I went through hell when I lost you,
I saw heaven when I found you,
I don't want to be possessive or sound a little too obsessive
But I just want to build my entire life around you.
You give the deaf sound, you give the blind sight,
You give the sick health, you even give the dead life.

Sometimes it's hard to trust you, and sometimes even harder to doubt you.

This may sound cliché, but I understand why they say

It's hard to live with you and even harder living without you.

I feel like when I have you I'm lucky,

You help me see the beauty in the ugly,

And you always make me see the better, that's why I want you here forever.

If you leave I'm hollow, if you lead I'll follow.

Although you're my girl I want to share you with the world—

Like just imagine what they could do with you in Chicago.

We've had a tumultuous relationship,

I want us to live harmoniously in love, without any hostility,

For you told me I could achieve as long as I believed that anything was a possibility.

You shined a bright light during dark nights,

You inspired me to see you in everything,

And every day you're mending me,

That's why I'm on a bending knee, asking you to accept this wedding ring.

I don't want to be solo, I'm thinking we should elope,

Kuz I learned from the 2015 U.S. Women's Soccer team

That you can't win or accomplish a dream without **hope**.

ROBERT (MOËT) COOVER

How-To

Did you finish your work? Put it in the bag—this is how you will have it ready. Put your bag by the door—this is how you will remember to take it with you. Lay out your clothes—this is how you will be ready for tomorrow. Now take a shower and put on your pajamas—this is how you will be ready for bed.

Wake up, go eat breakfast—this will give you energy for the day. Get dressed and brush your teeth. When you're done, I will help you do your hair—this will help you look your best for today.

We're leaving. See, I didn't even have to remind you to grab your bag 'cause it was by the door. A couple more times and this is how you get into a routine.

We're at your school. Keep your head high, I'll be here at three. And always know that I love you—this is how you'll be sure I'm never leaving you again and everything will be okay.

Thank you for the hug, but why so tight?

Because, Daddy, this is how you will now that I love you.

I Shall Not

I shall not be who I was yesterday nor content with who I am today, but I shall strive to be better than me tomorrow.

I shall no longer be the predator that the coupling of my environment and life circumstances has birthed. I shall be the positive opportunist who contributes to life's worth.

I shall not be a weed destroying the beauty in my yard. I shall be the weed repellant that allows the young plants to grow so that, little by little, my yard's beauty will begin to show.

I shall be the father I wish I had. I shall not be the definition of what I was shown it means to be a dad . . . or, I should say, lack thereof.

I shall not be who the majority believes me to be. I shall rise above—above my own undoing of negative ways due to optimistic views wrapped in pessimistic thoughts.

I shall be who I choose to be and not who I'm told I should be.

I shall be me, not who I am!

Podium

At first glance, it appears to be just a podium, pieces of metal and wood strung together and placed on a box. But if you look at it and think of the deeper meaning of what that podium represents, it will blow your mind. That podium is an outlet, a portal, it gives a person the chance to hold the attention of the room. It gives a person a place to present his goals, ideals, thoughts, and beliefs. That podium isn't just a podium—it's temporary freedom.

SOLOMON BOYD

Seward, Alaska

Write a poem in prison? Write a poem in prison?!
Who got time for that? Ain't no one got time for that.
Is it *hard*? What's easy about prison?
There's nothing easy in the jungle, this frozen tundra.
The dark nights carry long into the day.
No one wakes on the wrong side of the bed—
It's too small, there's only one side
No matter where you face your head.
Write a poem in prison? Do you mean
Like the eagles that soar above fearlessly?
Or the grizzly roaming the mountain range
Beckoning you to be one with nature and dare the elements,
Wishing you to jump that fence?
The clear blue sky with marshmallow clouds
And the green glacier mountain top
Sitting prominent as the cool breeze comes down
Through the forest on a hot summer day?
To stand and to see the scenery,
To taste the mountain spring water,
Is a slight piece of heaven,
More beautiful than streets of gold.
If Whitman had this view, what would *he* do?
But who got time for that? You didn't get time for that.
But thank God at least you see the beauty.
Some would die for it,
And you're alive. You just got time.
But for *this*?

Binky Boo

I wasn't there when you were born,
But you'll forgive me.
Because I wasn't there, I didn't name you—
Your mother's doing, but you'll forgive me.
You weren't christened Binky,
And I never knew what a Binky was till I met you.
I don't know why she called you Binky.
She was mad you looked just like me,
Then she held you and forgot her pain.
And I get it—no matter how bad, sad,
Or angry I was feeling,
I felt only joy holding you.
I'd bite your toes,
Blow whoopies on your belly,
Nibble on your ear,
Kiss you everywhere.
You were the sweetest baby.
We acquired rats somehow—
Apparently they were attracted to you,
Only fiddling with your dirty clothes.
You were the sweetest baby.
Even the dog would eat your diaper.
Your mother calls me Boo Boo
And I call your mother Boo Boo,
But I call you Binky Boo.
When you happily passed gas, I called you Stinky Boo.
When you ripped off your Pamper and drew on the wall with poop,
I called you Poody Boo.
When you put the dog food in your mouth, I called you Scooby Boo.
No matter what you did or do, in the end
You're my Boo.
Binky Boo.

King of Hoarders

You got a cold, I got a pill,
Got a rag for every spill.
You want to blow your nose, I got a tissue.
What's the issue?
I'm the King of Hoarders.
I got every baseball card from 1951,
Even got the gum.
This guy here, like most of them
His rookie year he was a bum,
His second year, though—50 home runs.
After millions of dollars, he'll now tell you
Steroids is dumb.
His name is Mark McGwire.
I'm the King of Hoarders.
I went hunting because I want a deer on the wall,
And a bear on the floor,
And a bear on my back.
But I can't bear to see all this meat go to waste
So I bought three freezers—
And I'm a vegetarian.
I'm the King of Hoarders.
I may be broke, but that's a joke,
I got a house with a junkyard in the back yard,
Old cars look like junk,
Got trunks in the trunk,
Inside the trunks, more junk, like boxes,
Inside the boxes, bags,
Inside the bags, rocks—
You know, the shiny ones you hold onto forever.
I'm going to send my daughter to university,
She's going to be a doctor.
Yeah, I'm the King of Hoarders.

Advice

I dream of the day when I joyously give you away,
with a little reluctance in my heart because I want you to stay,
and because I know of the price that you may have to pay.

Do not be afraid to wait for something that is no less than great.
Every morning when you wake you should be greeted with a kiss;
when he leaves the house, you should be left with a kiss,
with a look in his eyes reflecting the hours he will surely miss.

God forbid that he sin, but God forgives man,
and he should worship you next to God.
If he falters, have it in your heart to forgive him, because you can.

If he feels you're a thorn in his side and he expresses doubt,
think of my unwavering love for your mother and tell him to pluck
you out.

Measure the strength of his heart by the way he speaks
at the end of every conversation, with words of venom or sweet.
If his last words are not "I love you," then his love and devotion
are weak.

For sickness and in health, in case you poison him.
Till death do you part, in case you put him in prison.
For richer or poorer, in case you take everything.

He should still confess that he loves you
and honor the vow to never leave you for another.
But I advise you, he will love you so much more
if you don't act like your mother.

I Know, I Know

Incoherently, the words kept coming, a smorgasbord of sweet, savory, and bitter, of memories and desires to be filled. Helplessly, I parroted what I heard:

"You want me to feed the dog . . . Don't give that bitch nothing . . . I remember, I remember—she bit you . . . You love him so . . . He's your only son . . . We all said he was your favorite . . . Yes, yes, he's going to be a minister, as soon as he gets out of prison."

After thrashing back and forth like a hurricane, the calm of the eye of the storm rests with breathless silence. Holding your hand so lifeless, I anticipated another seizure to let me know you're still with me.

Eyes open and movement of fingers like a gentle caressing hug. With the strength and power of knowing that tomorrow we'll be here, a new resolve to finish what is started. Though the pain has subsided, there's no cure. Distraught with the thought of the inevitable, the only original words I can utter: "I know, I know."

The Little Monk

Little Brucey on Saturday afternoon. They showed old karate flix every week. He emulates everything he sees. He yells back, "Ma, I'm doing my pushups. I have to do 1,000. One hundred . . . Two hundred . . ." He grunts loud enough so that we can all hear. He jumps up and down on the bed to get as much height as he can and finally does a flying kick from one bed to the next. "Flying drop kick," he explains in a comical supposed Chinese accent. When I glimpse this, I wonder how often he has practiced this.

At dinner, he sits cross-legged in his chair at the table and exercises his strength and speed over his little sister and yells, "Eagle claw!" as he grabs her little fingers reaching for a chicken leg. "Son-say eats first, yun-one."

He dresses in a kimono with a flaming dragon and a black bear, and after every movie he immediately turns to me and bows, then shouts, "Eeee-ya!" and hops into a fighting stance.

Sometimes I engage, but one sunny Saturday I was a little tired. I suggested he go outside and play. He returned not long after with a welt on his cheek.

"What's this?" I asked.

Spiritedly he quoted his favorite movie, *Enter the 36ᵗʰ Chamber*: "My technique must improve. I should never lose to Tommy."

"Tommy is nine and a half, and you're only seven," I tell him.

"Wu Tang can't beat Shaolin Ma! Didn't you see the movie? I am Shaolin!"

The Persuader

We weren't necessarily the most unruly bunch of kids—it's hard to tell from the perspective of a child—but we spoke vulgar language fluently while stuttering improper English in the presence of adults, and we may have broken a lamp or drinking glass every so often, or mischievously snuck a piece of cake or cookie while playing in the house, which was not allowed. And so, once a month, there was a festive moment when the whole household gathered together for what was described as P.G. Day—Parental Guidance Day. On this day, free of charge to anyone's account, the Persuader came out—a thick, black, rawhide leather belt. We were unconcerned with its high quality; we only knew it was so tough it could likely suspend a small car. When the Persuader came out, you had broken the rules, crossed the line, said or did something, and it was time to pay up. You were going to get your butt whooped. Being the youngest and smallest, I don't think little Mikey understood or comprehended the purpose of P.G. Day. Looking back, I'm not sure I did either. But Mikey had a mortal fear of the Persuader, so that the slightest mention would grab all his attention, and he would straighten his collar, tie his shoes. The sight of it would open the flood gates and send him scampering with reckless abandon in every direction. But running only infuriated a most stubborn matriarch. It was viewed as disobedient and disrespectful. If you were told to stick your hand out or turn around and bend over, you did it. To do otherwise, there was double the licking for one's attitude. Though Mammy was stubborn, she was just, and being that no one was technically guilty of any act on this joyful occasion, if willing, one could step forward on behalf of another. But if little Mikey ran, it would be a double portion for whoever chose it. Heroically, I would step forward, and every month we'd watch to see if Mikey stayed put, and every month he ran. It came to where he'd just look at me and I'd walk in front of

Mammy and say, "I'll take Mikey's portion." To this day, Mikey has never owned or worn a piece of leather, not even a shoe. He says it's something about the smell that disturbs him. And I have never owned a leather belt. Occasionally, I have had leather jackets, but none that I was ever so thrilled about. They were given to me as gifts, which I accepted. I still have the Persuader though, and I have yet to come across another leather that I felt was worthy or would stand the test of time. I have gifted the belt to my daughter. She is only ten years old. Surprisingly, it fits her. Though the quality is very expensive, it's a child's belt, and even now she looks forward to a time when she is the head of a household and tasked with persuading her little ones. She is not afraid of the Persuader. Though I saved Mikey from an unfortunate experience, it baffles me that my little princess wishes to carry on the tradition. I certainly did not persuade her.

Poetry, Poetry, Poetry

Poetry is the language of the heart,
of convictions, deep-down rooted belief
learned from God,
from mouth to ear,
through generations.

An ambiguous song, a piano concerto
with lyrics inspired by the beats of life,
translated from a foreign tongue into a universal language.

Poetry is what you see, hear, feel.
Hands up. Don't shoot.
Gun in my pocket. Drugs in the car.
I'm not Black. Lives don't matter.
Money is power. Bittersweet.
Stench of death.
The sixth sense speaks; it's not you talking.

Poetry is love. Flowers
in the hands of a brute.
Perfumed fragrance too strong
even for a broken nose.
From a Cinderella with a trampled embroidered train
held by seven dwarves.

Poetry is never wrong.
It is an agreement of the soul.
To dance freely out of rhythm
to the sounds of crickets, ocean tides, avalanches.

Poetry is nothing,
but everything and anything,
if something to you.

This One is for Binky

May you raise a son to be better than his father
and his father's fathers. May he be a good husband
and a good father and always speak of the loving
bond between you and him.

May you be dressed in all white with a long train
and your eyes sparkle more than a diamond
as you lift the veil in a church with
a steeple surrounded by family and friends of old and to be.

May you know the heart of a man when you bury
your face in the pillow to muffle the pain
of some foolish boy after school, and then remember
the warm embracing hugs and kisses that comforted you when
you cried out as a child, and know you're always loved.

May you smile unknowingly when you hear the key of G,
an unexpected flutter of your heart moves
you side to side, in step with the music of *The Wizard of Oz*.

May you eat with your fingers and enjoy being fed
and share your food with those you like
and occasionally prompt a food fight with those you don't.

May you run before you walk and laugh when you
fall and learn to stand on your own, never
depending on a hand to hold you up.

May you never be ashamed to be helped to clean up
a mess you made, and may you always smell the roses
because everything about you is sweet.

May you never forget the greatest love you have,
from the father you once had.

Untitled

My
life,
it suc
ks, but
I'm no
sucker.
That's a
real big
joke. Suc
kers get to
have all the
fun. Their
food is al
ways alive.
Mine is alive,
but I'm no suck
er. I bite, but
then I just s
wallow. W
here is the
thrill in that?
The glands
in my mouth
are not taste
buds. When I
open my mou
th, that docile
little mouse is
going to walk
right in it. And

there's no grass.
There's no deceit
ful and cunning
attack. I don't
even have to
coil up to stri
ke. At least
when people
look at me
they are
still intim
idated. I
am go
ing
to   bite.

The Pen and the Sword

I write and I write and I write.
I am convinced that I was heard
and that what I said was just. And yet. And yet!

What good are you, pen, if no one will listen?

I write the law. I'm the power behind
the letter of the law.
They turn to me when the final decisions are made,
and with my assistance they execute judgment.
But what do I do when they won't listen?

Turn to me, I will give you refuge.
I will make them listen.
I will force them to think before they act.

Heed him not. Those who live by the sword
die by the sword.
He is all-consuming.
All includes you.

I'm ordained with innate authority, from
commandments to amendments.
They don't carry me in vain.
I'm the power behind the pen,
and I am the executioner of judgment.

I'm mightier than the sword!

Only if they listen.

Back and forth they went.
I am mightier than the sword!
Only if they listen.
I am mightier than the sword!

Only if they listen . . .

Black American

At times, I like to express my mind.
I'm grateful this ain't North Korea, because it would be a crime.
I like to confront perceived established lies;
in some other country for that I might die.
In this great country for protesting I might just pay a fine,
unless you're black with a prior record likely to do felony time.
But if you're rich or white, all will be fine.
I think to myself on this Fourth of July,
how all the people sing aloud with American pride;
I reflect back on the day when our national anthem was made—
did they think of me and how I, a black man, was made?
I dream of the day when there will be no "African-American"—
just American.
When that day comes, I will encourage my brothers and sisters to
sing again,
but I think not ill of those who now still can,
for every now and then I myself sing that song,
whether it be because I like the melody or to just get along.
But I am privy to the fact that repetition has led me to condone
that song
when there are parts that I know are clearly wrong.
I will not lie, no matter how much I try;
I cannot forget what it means to be black in America, even on the
Fourth of July.
I am very grateful, though conflicted, on American pride.
I believe this is the greatest nation on earth—
if I saw one better, I'd be surprised.
So when the fireworks go off and light up the sky on any Fourth of July,
don't be confused if you see me hoot and cheer,
for, after all, I was still born and raised here.

EXODUS COOKE

Toy Soldier

I can remember as a tot how I always wished for a toy soldier the way one who's in the desert desires water. Every time I seen the action figure on TV, I felt I was one step closer to my dream. I'd watch as it twisted, turned, kicked, punched, wondering when I would have my shot to make it split, karate chop, back flip. There were times I caught myself salivating for this ice cream cone dream to be a reality.

The day soon came when the toy soldier would be mine. But I must admit I gave up on it at a time when I felt my mama turned a blind eye to this true desire I had. She just didn't know how badly I wanted the action figure. I tried to explain it to her in adult language, but when I said it's like Auntie, who said all the time she loves a man to be eating with her—that's how much I wanted my toy—oh boy, Mama just looked at me, smiled, then started laughing. I didn't know what was so funny, so as a giant elephant I went to my room with tears in my eyes.

Days later, Mama called me to her room. I had forgotten about the toy and moved on to the infinite ends of space, where the limits are limitless. Rushing to Mama, I hopped onto her lap. She asked me did I know what she had. Staring at her face, I seen she had new glasses and I stated such. She said, "That's my li'l man, always paying attention. But that's not what I'm talking about." She reached behind her and brought forth a box.

I grasped and opened it. I yelled, "Moooommmm, this box is empty!"

She said, "Is it really?"

"Yeah, see?" I said and showed her the empty box.

She smiled, then said, "It's not empty."

Puzzled, I said, "It's not?" Then I turned the box upside down and shook it.

Mama said, "It has air in it."

All I could do was stare at her. "Funny, Mom."

As I was about to descend from her lap, she started to tickle me. Trying to stay mad, I screamed, "Nope, nope, nope!" But I couldn't help laughing. Finally, she stopped, looked at me, reached behind herself once more and gave me another box, larger than the first. I thought, Oh boy, she's trying to trick me again. I shook it and it appeared to have something inside. I looked at Mama with a devilish grin on her face, like a sneaky evil elf. I squinted my eyes, squished my face, and shook the box once more. Hearing something move, I tore the box open and was Medusa'd, my mouth and eyes wide open in amazement. I boa constrictored Mama, showing her my love. With fireworks going off in my body, I looked again in the box, and there it was, my toy soldier.

Ode to My Pops

A man who was quiet yet thunderous
And truly a whirlwind of wisdom;
Whose thoughts of others were wondrous,
Kindness to all who crossed his path succumb.

He was genuinely gentle, but stern,
Unmoving in his demeanor, though not rude;
Shake of the hand was vise-grip firm,
Stable in providing for his brood.

Considered a giant among his peers,
One who was not given to ill acts;
Never terrified, for a man of few fears,
Always had his family and friends' backs.

My father had many trips and falls;
Yes, my dad did always stand through it all.

Love Thy Enemy

My archenemy, an enraged psychopath, was at death's door,
Beating on it with the ferocity of a caged gorilla behind a steel door.
Never did I think I would have the opportunity to gloat over
Her being so close to being in a closed casket, life over.

I stood above her with a joyous grin, yet weighed down with a heavy heart,
For I believed when came the day of her demise I'd have a cold heart.
But as I looked on her frail condition, my emotions no longer frost bitten
Toward her—anger, rage, animosity gone—by kindness I was now bitten.

After all the years of trying to annihilate one another, being the other's pain,
I found myself gravitating toward peace, wanting to ease her pain.
I grasped her hand and she looked upon me as a dearly beloved friend,
With a slight smirk—in that she acknowledged that I was the furthest
thing from a friend.

With the end of a war we both hated to love, we came to grips,
Knowing at this moment that my hand may be the last she grips.

A Drunk Man's Tale: Am I a Drunk?

Before daylight, the night is always electric. Bars are full of people who are, of course, drunk. One night I went to a bar, got drunk, and watched this one girl with a purse on the table. Every time she moved the drink, she slopped it onto the purse. Another girl, in this same bar, continued spilling the drink she had all over the purse every time she tried to drink it. Another time I got drunk at a different bar that had a bright light on its terrace. I watched as this one client, an old man who, once drunk, would talk to the bright light. The waiters knew him well, and before it got too late a waiter would have a guard get the old man's young wife, who lived over the bar. There was another bar I went to to get drunk, with the name *Kingdom*. Its bar counter had leather covering, as did its tables. The waiters would give coffee half past every other hour to those who may want it. The drunken people never took it but always asked for another drink. You know, the thing about many drunk people: they never know when they are drunk. The day after, we are hung over and have another drink.

I once asked this question: How do drunk people stay with a job? Answer: They are not drunk at work. Although we might drink at work, we are never drunk on the job. Well, some of us are not. I was thinking about this as I sat at a bar counter with an empty brandy bottle and an empty glass. I motioned for the barman to deliver another full bottle. What? What did you expect? I'm a drunk, and I'm not a drunk. Trying to get there. You know what, you'll know before I do anyway when I'm drunk. Hell, an old colleague once said to me, she does not know how my wife put up with me. I said, "That is why she is not my wife, because I wouldn't be putting up with what she had to say." She smiled. Anyway, she didn't know what she was talking about. We drunk people are probably the only kind people. Some people may know, provided you get us drunk. When I was younger, people would tell me that it is not necessary for me to be drunk to be kind. I always agreed. Of course, I would be drunk when I did so.

People, people, people: Never pressure a drunk to stop. You do that, then he, or she, will need a drink to get away from the pressure. You understand how that works. If not, I will tell you, but I need a drink. Bottle, glass, drink, poured—everything in its place! I'm all settled. Let me tell you about a drunk like me. Well, not a drunk but a man who likes to drink. I don't drink because I'm a drunk; I'm a drunk because I drink. I don't need a good bottle of brandy. I *want* a good bottle of brandy. You understand me? You get the difference? Of course you do!

Look at the wife. One thing she does to pressure me is to always have our beautiful little niece tell me not to drink. One day when she said this to me, I said, "I don't tell you what to do, and you don't tell me what to do. Agreed?" She looked at me, turned and looked back at me once more, then ran to the wife. About two minutes went by before she came back with a saucer and cup. She stood by me, waiting for me to look. Slowly I turned and she smiled at me.

"Will you have coffee with me?"

"What did I tell you?"

"I *asked* you this time."

"Well, you can't have coffee!"

Thinking for a long time, she finally said, "Will you drink the coffee if I sit with you?"

This little girl was not going to give up. I took the saucer and cup that was full of steam and drank the coffee. "Now leave me be."

She ran back to the wife. "He drunk it."

I went back to the half-empty glass of brandy I had. The pressure the little girl put on me made me need a drink.

So, people, know and understand that if you want a drunk to clean himself up, don't pressure him. Am I drunk? No. Then again, probably. No, certainly not. Then again, let me have a drink while I'm thinking about it.

QUAN A. SOYINI

Love

You're the worst
You feel good
And you hurt
You heal
Then get me killed
You get to be too much
And at times you're not enough
With friends like you, who needs enemies?
With love like this, who needs anything?
I shout you out so the world can see
I regret I told you, silly me
I hate you

Rapture

I was shopping for sneakers one day and came across a street vendor. He had quite a few items that piqued my interest, especially this CD. I picked it up like it was a rare jewel or a delicate artifact. My mom used to love this CD. Wow, Anita Baker's *Rapture*. I flipped it to the back, then to the front again. It was as if the CD was a key to my memory vault 'cause just like a near death experience, all the precious time my mother walked this earth flashed through my mind. I cracked a smile as I envisioned her doing her signature dance as Anita sang. I shuddered as the feeling of unconditional love she blanketed me and my siblings with all our life engulfed me, as if she was standing right there. I looked behind me 'cause the feeling was that strong. I asked the vendor how much for the CD. He said five bucks. I handed him a twenty and headed to my car. As I sat in my car, I continued to look at Anita on the cover and started to see my mom's face. I shed a tear, put the CD in, and sang along with Anita as I pulled off. Rest in peace, Mom.

MAX WELL

Jailhouse Mirror

Looking in the mirror
through these addicted eyes,
I see a gaunt, sad face
looking back at me
through lines of coke and heroin
that I snort to not feel the pain.
I throw the mirror in anger,
it shatters on the floor,
I see my face in pieces
in a pile on the floor.
My face looks like a Picasso canvas,
my life feels just the same.
The pain I've caused my loved ones
gives me guilt, remorse, and shame.
   Years go by as I avoid
    the mirror of my life.
Now I'm looking into the stainless
steel mirror on the wall above my sink.
Looking at me is a blurry face,
so I tape my jailhouse mirror
to the stainless steel.
I see an old vacant face
staring back at me.
His eyes are sunken,
his cheeks are hollow,
as I wonder how others feel,
looking in their jailhouse mirror.

The Snake Within

There is a snake within me,
Coiled and ready to strike!
I keep it at bay deep inside me,
It feeds on my anger and pain.
So I inject a milky white substance
That keeps me mellow and numb.
The snake hisses, then nods—
He's sated, at least for today.
But I can't keep living this way!

There is a snake within me,
Coiled and ready to strike!
When I get angry, I set him free.
He spits out poisonous venom
At my family, loved ones, and friends.
I hear him cursing and swearing,
Ready to strike, to cause hurt and pain.
I calm myself and stuff him back in!

There is a snake within me,
Coiled and ready to strike!
We have to live together
Or I will go insane!
I put away the needle,
I have to do this clean.
I go deep into the forest and curse, swear, and scream
Till I open my mouth and nothing comes out.
I've let out a lifetime of anger and pain.
The snake within me smiles.
I smile and hold him tight.
I've learned not to push him down
But to let him out slowly,
So the anger doesn't turn to pain.

Three Haiku

Trout jumps at a fly
Fisherman sets the hook and cries
Trout released and swims away

Behind my masks you see
What you want me to be but
I don't even know me

Water falls from streams
Weeping willow tree waves and sways
Pop goes the cell door—I sigh

Me, My Cell, and I

The anger   erupts like a
volcano.   Bile spews
from   me as I sit
in my   cell, my mind
spiraling   down as
I feel the   pain I've caused
my loved   ones, like a tornado
that's about   to hit ground and cause
chaos to   everyone I touch.
Like a   hurricane landing on shore
causing   tears to spray from my eyes,
the hurri   cane tossing boats, smashing
them against   houses, people yelling and
screaming   in my cell,
tearing   things apart. Like those poor people
I feel   the sadness dragging me down
as I   put my hands on my face and cry,
I feel   the calm before the storm.
In it   there's losses all around:
my   freedom, humility, time, the list
goes on   and on. Then the storm hits
and I feel   like dying, so I
curl up in the   fetal position till the
storm rages   past, as I try to let
go, as I shout   out loud, "When is my
rainbow going to come?!"

The Weeping Willow Tree and Me

The weeping willow tree that stood majestically in my backyard before I was even born.

The willow tree that I tried to climb at the age of three but fell and skinned my knee.

The willow tree that I could see from my bed at night when the moon was right, swayed to and

fro and scared me, so I would pull the covers over my head to shelter me from dread!

The willow tree that I wept in and under.

The willow tree where I played under the shade of, with dinosaurs and Army men doing battle.

The willow tree with weeping branches, which I swung on like vines, giving my best Tarzan whine.

The willow tree that ate some kites and balloons.

The willow tree that I'd sit in and listen to the Yankees game on my transistor radio.

The willow tree that made me weep when I fell out of it and broke my arm.

The willow tree that ate up the Whiffle balls my brother or I would hit, that ended the game.

The willow tree whose trunk was as big as a car.

The willow tree that I'd climb to the top of on early mornings and late afternoons to see the sun

rise and set with beautiful colors.

The willow tree that I carved my initials into then added a girlfriend's initials when I was nine or ten—not sure when it was—*KM+SP.*

The willow tree that my friends and I would camp under.

The willow tree that as I grew older the branches would not hold me.

The willow tree that throughout the years broke bones, cuts, scrapes, and left some scars.

The willow tree that fell mightily, taking the shed and the pool with it, during the hurricane of '71, I watched from a window as a tear fell from my eye.

233

ANDY M.T.

A Reflections' Past

A hundred eyes stare back at me as my fist bleeds in beautiful agony. Mocking me. Making fun of me. Laughing. They refuse to speak even though one eye can speak a thousand more words than two lips could ever put together.

The man I saw was no man at all. Trapped in a glass prison, screaming in pain, struggling in chains, begging me to set him free. I tried walking away but I could always hear him. Every time I looked, he was casting his stones at me, but like a strange optical illusion the stones would seem as if they were being thrown toward him. I couldn't take it anymore, so I threw a punch.

The spider web cracks before me only compliment the spider web of lies I've tangled myself in. My face looks like what it might if I don't get out of here soon: old, broken, disturbed, permanent. After all, I am no Dorian Gray. I can feel the sharp edges on my fingertips as I caress the new portrait. And even though I'm gone, I know I'm still there.

Mirrors are no blank canvas but for the minds that choose to see them as one. The reflections we see are not merely the objects we put in front of them but the ideas that remain behind them—ideas that are closer than they appear.

I will not be taken advantage of.

I will not be taking advantage.

Unrequited Sin

These walls are closing in today
I don't know how I lost my way
The Lord, I'm sure, is very near
If He could see I'm lost, I pray

Down on my knees I shed a tear
It drips, it falls, it lands in beer
And though I know I'll never know
The Grace of God is what I fear

These walls are closing in—oh no!
I don't know where I'm s'posed to go
I cannot breathe, I cannot see
I feel like Edgar Allen Poe

Her heart it sits under a tree
The beat it makes, that is my plea
Do I deserve to be set free?
Do I deserve to be set free?

What I've Done

I once gave a cousin of mine $700 to buy a new car;
A year later, the car was repossessed.
I once spent $300 on groceries for a neighbor;
I went hungry that night because I had no food in my own cabinets.
I once spent $800 for my stepmother to move into a new apartment;
A month later, she flew across the country to live with a guy she had never met.
I once spent $1,500 to move my real mother to another state so she could be with my sister and her grandchildren;
I never told her how much I still need her here with me.
I once gave $20 to a man at the bus station who needed to see his mother;
Five minutes later he came back and asked for more money.
I once paid for an older lady's meal when she didn't have enough money herself;
When I asked if I could dine with her, she said she'd rather eat alone.
I once stayed up all night helping a girlfriend with a college assignment;
She got an "A" and then slept with my roommate.
I once punched a guy for stealing something from a girl I had a crush on;
She wouldn't give me her number.
I once taught some kids how to survive in the wilderness;
They later burned down the forest.
I once taught a man how to cook for himself;
He burned himself in the fire.
I once taught a man how to fish;
He drowned himself in the lake.
I once taught someone how to drive a 5-speed;
After one day they blew the clutch.
I once taught a man how not to kill someone for revenge;
He eventually stabbed me in the back.
When somebody asks me for help because they are in need,
I hope they understand that I'm in need of some help for myself.

The Love of a Rose

Your love for me is like a rose
      Beautiful and sweet-smelling
           Tall as forever goes.
My love for you is like the soil
      Dark and rich
           Your roots deep inside me.
Your love for me is like a rose
      The thorns on which I grab
           And there on you I bleed.
My love for you is like the rain
      Cleansing and refreshing
           Hydrating, you drink me.
Your love for me is like a rose
      Your petals bloom in glorious life
           Your petals fall in glorious death.
My love for you is like the sun
      Bright and shining
           Warmth without a fire.
Your love for me is like a rose
      Your roots reaching far underground
           Sucking the life of all it can bear.
My love for you is like a rose
      It grows and it wilts
           It blossoms and it folds.
My love for you is perennial
      Your love for me is pristine.
Our love is together forever
      Our love is our own.

AKHIVELLI

Remember . . . Before She Bore U

PEACE.

Remember . . . before she bore U I adored U,
Stressing on how we would support U,
Feeling the pain as I think of a name to call U.

Before U, liquor was my baby. It was all that I needed.
I would drink that poison until I felt completed.
I would drink that poison until I felt conceited.
I would drink that poison until, finally, I was defeated.
I would drink poison and rejoice in the choice to get bent.
Now babies drink poison without a choice, or consent.
I think it's time we repent.
As I think of U now, I'm reminded of the name *Flint*.

Remember . . . before she bore U I adored U,
Stressing on how we would support U,
Feeling the pain as I think of a name to call U.

Your mother's womb is your home,
Now U wanna be free, my little refugee,
Free from the sounds of hand grenades,
Free from the sounds of helicopter blades,
Free from the sounds of AK-47s that rattle off while people say
Alhamdulillah—translated, To Allah Be the Praise.
Man, what a phrase.
I know U would trade tyranny for security.
You're welcomed to America.
As I think of U now, I'm reminded of the name *Syria*.

Remember . . . before she bore U I adored U,
Stressing on how we would support U,
Feeling the pain as I think of a name to call U.

It's strange, living in a land that's occupied by "The Man,"
Who needs to be forced to understand
That BLACK LIVES MATTER.
So I wonder what would be the MATTER
My unborn BLACK child will face trying to LIVE.
Will a hoodie get him killed?
For his safety, anything I would give.
Several shots didn't make him stop,
He thought he did no harm.
As I think of U now, I'm reminded of the name *Trayvon*.
Remember . . . before she bore U I adored U,
Stressing on how we would support U,
Feeling the pain as I think of a name to call U.

Nine months have come and gone.
You're here, my dear, optimistic as the sun brightly shining.
As I look at U now, I'm deeply reminded,
Reminded of the past so that your future doesn't suffer the same fate.
So it's important that I feel justice when saying your name,
Justice for their sake.
'cause now she bore U, and God knows I adore U,
forgetting all that made me stress on how we would support U,
feeling the pain as I give U this name:
Dhakara.
Yeah, Dhakara is what they'll call U,
The Arabic word for *Remember*.
So, remember, Dhakara,
That Daddy loves U, and I'll do anything for U.

PEACE.

Tattle-Tale, Preach!

PEACE.

Hey call me a tattle-tale because I'm a truth-speaker.
So now they mad as hell, but I speak the truth for
the truth-seeker—PEEP!

Jack and Jill went up the hill to cop a bag of dope.
Jack and Jill came back down the hill,
Now their parents don't know how to cope.
It's amazing how . . . people in this society live in denyingly
About the drug epidemic until it's thrown on their front porch
in variety.
And I don't mean the magazine—I mean the white average teen.
Nobody cared when black folks was crack folks.
To me it's all a massive scheme.
PREACH!

They call me a tattle-tale because I'm a truth-speaker,
So now they mad as hell, but I speak the truth for
the truth-seeker—PEEP!

Here's something they don't want me to speak of,
Like . . . how Meka was a freaka, now she got sexually-transmitted Zika?
They want to blame it on the Brazilians—
Indeed, a brilliant scheme.
You being lied to.
Let me tell you about these so-called diseases:
AIDS, Ebola, and the swine flu . . .
I think it's time to put you on to the greatest secret never told,
Like how your TV station lies to your faces about the CDC plan
For population control.
PREACH!

They call me a tattle-tale because I'm a truth-speaker,
So now they mad as hell, but I speak the truth for the truth-seeker—PEEP!

Democrats and Republicans—they're your real Bloods and Crips,
Gangbangin', campaignin' for the government.
OK, so let's address the Elephant in the room:
Truth is, they all a bunch of Jackasses,
How they separate us with their lower, middle, and upper classes,
Federal tactics, build and destroy is the ploy they apply,
And if you ask your Congress, then surely they'll deny,
So the truth I supply.
Keep a CBS on their behavior because one black man
Who's president of this land
Will not be your savior.
And this ain't a black and white thing,
It's a facts of life thing,
So I speak the truth because it's just,
And it's only the right thing.
PREACH!

So call me a tattle-tale.
I'll keep being a truth-speaker so long as there's a truth to be told,
Along with a truth-seeker.
So, who wants to hear the truth?

PEACE.

Still Life of a Rose

PEACE!
Despite the concrete, in the alley of a dark street,
This rose had the will and still rose with a heartbeat.
Now watch this beautiful rose,
Like Tyra, strike a beautiful pose.
Soon the petals will leave,
Maybe like a new model trying to get ahead,
So instead of working hard, it chose to disrobe.
Ambition, I suppose.
See, for this rose, hope SPRINGS eternal
Because its beauty makes the eyes admire
What hearts desire.
Love flings can last a lifetime until the SUMMER.
Time then after will have the physical beauty
Of this rose, like trodden roads expired.
But until then, watch it stand tall with pride,
Because, after all, that usually comes before the FALL,
Then it's death during the WINTER.
So, just remember the rose for what it was worth,
Understanding that love's trials are substantial,
Like the thorns on the stem,
So, to appreciate the beautiful petals,
Love will hurt.
And maybe the best year is next year.
May it be eternal, like God's speech.
And pray that she is it,
The beautiful rose that grows from the concrete.
PEACE!

Like Water, For Lily to Grow

PEACE.
What I'm about to say
seems silly, I know,
but just consider it "like water, for Lily to grow."
Specially unexpected,
your pops planted a seed
into "the Earth,"
so before your birth I was besieged
by thoughts of my faults,
but now they serve as light,
so I'll quench your thirst
with words like water to succeed,
assuming you've heard them right.
Keep your friends close to you,
but more importantly, your friendliest foes,
because they'll always be lurking,
and soon enough that envy will show.
Forget "try"—do your best,
because that will keep away regretting.
If you fail, it's a lesson to be learned,
so therein lies the blessing.
Should you succeed,
be humble,
the same as when you stumble,
because pressure busts pipes,
but it also makes a diamond.
Since your birth I knew your worth,
because I've always seen you shining.
Love what you come from,
that mixed, rich, black, beautiful soil,

because it's the ground that helps you grow,
so to it, know to always be loyal.
Keep your word,
because your word is your bond,
and your bond is your life.
Say what you mean,
just don't be mean when you say it,
because there is no blameworthiness in being polite.
If you wrong someone,
put pride aside and make it right.
These guys will try to run game,
but can't you see, like an amputee,
they don't have a leg to stand on.
That's clowns fooling around,
but they'll disguise it as them
"just getting their grown man on."
Peer pressure will nudge you,
but never live life to please another's sight,
because there's only one God that can judge you.
Know that I love you,
so I give you this knowledge,
and it's plenty to know.
But for now, from me to you,
this is "like water, for Lily to grow."
Grow strong.
Grow wise.
PEACE.

Stix-n-Stonez

PEACE.
Stix-n-stonez can break my bonez,
But if I catch 'em, then F 'em,
Because even before my conception,
To them I was known as the "N word."
But now they find ways to say it behind my back,
As if it's not the same crap my ancestors heard.
So I roll wit' the punches like the wheels
On the chariot of Ben-Hur,
Because liars know the truth can't be
Censored from the sensei.
Now watch me block every shot they take at me
Like I'm Dikembe,
And I'm proud to be descended from Kunta Kinte,
Or even Kensay,
So "give us-us free" and let me be,
Because you can't give a God-given right, right?
And your wrong is only as strong as I let it be,
So, if you hate me, then know that
I came before U,
Like C descended from the letter B,
And I pray to the letter A because
"He" has always been before us all.
That's d-e-f-initely capital G . . . God.
Stix-n-stonez can break my bonez,
But only He can take my soul,
So let he without sin cast the first stone with pride.
But if it's me versus Hate,
Then let's take ten and spin,
And he who flash the first chrome survives . . .

BOOM!
There's no room for a Black Muslim
When there's a man who wants to repeal,
Replace, and push 'em off a land
Where his greatest grands used their bare hands
To pick that cotton from them bushes.
But the former first recited a verse that replied,
"When they go low, we go high."
So, can you see me hovering over your despicable utterance?
That's got you trapped because of your stubbornness.
So, say what you say,
I'm just a listener,
I realize they got new ways of calling me the "N word,"
The new word as I know it is
"The Black Prisoner."
So go ahead, stop and frisk,
Search and murder me.
Stix-n-stonez can break my bonez,
But my will will never allow your hateful words
To continue hurting me.
I. AM. BLACK!
So you're just gonna have to live with that.
PEACE.

Here Today, Gone Tomorrow

PEACE.
Here today, gone tomorrow,
but when tomorrow becomes yesterday,
leaving U stressed today,
there's only pain and sorrow,
and for the pain, a tough pill to swallow.
Recently
I lost a piece of my decency departed,
dearly beloved.
But I'm here, my dear,
I'm finally here,
'cause in life,
my cousin's life
helped my cause . . . in life.
So why should the sun set on a son who left just as much light?
Without him, if the future's bright,
I can't see it!
So, am I blind then?
When my hindsight is two times ten
plus that
knowing God is great with fate,
to find relief, I have to trust that.
Ironically, I broke my cousin's Transformer when I was a boy,
and he never asked any questions.
It was always the same with me
in regards to his affection.
He was authentic,
and if he's a sign, then God sent it as a blessing.
There's not enough water in the world that could be shed
for my dead . . . so I'll pray.

Because if he was here on tomorrow's yesterday
he would say,
"Remember me at my best,
forgive me at my worst,
love is love, li'l cuz,
so remember that, for what it's worth."
So, yesterday I missed you,
today I miss you,
tomorrow . . . I'll miss you.
Here today, gone tomorrow,
but when tomorrow becomes yesterday,
leaving U stressed today,
there's only pain and sorrow,
and for the pain, a tough pill to swallow.
Recently
I lost a piece of my decency departed,
dearly beloved.
But I'm here, my dear,
I'm finally here.
Thanks, cuz.
Love is love.
PEACE.

Dedicated to Aron and Sidney. You'll be missed.

My Free Dome

PEACE.
MY FREEDOM! MY FREEDOM!
MY! FREE! DOME!
So what does it cost for me to close my eyes . . .
and see home?
Because all I see are blind visions of Africa
While men pay their debt to society
From a prison called Attica
And overseers lash at the slave.
Who tries to abscond from the pain
That bonds 'em to the chains.
Praying they melt to swords
Used to slay the slave master
All the while seeking forgiveness from their Lord.
Because Lord knows—
There's no greater threat than a Negro with a knife
turned crook.
Or worse . . .
A Negro who knows how to read books.
Books that taught an "American Dream,"
Known to me as an American scheme.
Land stolen from the previous owners who had it
Woven into the fabric stitched with an American seam.
And it's not hard to see that it's far from hard luck.
When they kicked us outta Starbucks
And all I ordered was a large cup of Black Freedom.
And instead you gave me free doom!
Then assumed I wouldn't make it.
But here's a missive to massa—
Prepare for your disaster because I was born to take it

And they stated—
"Life is like a box of Lupita dark skin"
And if history has a way of being repeated
Watch me defeat it—
Because we're never going back to pickin' cotton again!
I pick MY FREEDOM! MY FREE DOME!
MY! FREE! DOME!
So what does it cost me to close my eyes . . .
and see home?
Because all I see is a bunch of young Nat Turners
Who clap burners
Raising the crime rate
Every time there's a Black murder
And white earners laugh
Because we lack learnin' from our past.
And when asked why'd I do it—
Would you believe me like Sethe
If I said I only killed my "Beloved"
Because the "Devil" was tuggin' away my heart.
Scratching my head thinking—
"Better I than the Po-lice in this cold life"
From who I only ever knew—
WHIPS AND CHAINS!
WHIPS AND CHAINS!
WHIPS AND CHAINS!
Till finally all I ever desired—
Was a brand new "whip and chain."
Strange, I know, but let me put in it its proper tense:
The stench of piss sticks
Till someone sees fit for a proper verse.
Now does it make sense?
So I guess the "moral" of the horror

Is like Cora the explorer on "The Underground Railroad"—
I'm just in pursuit of MY FREEDOM! MY FREEDOM!
MY! FREE! DOME!—
So what does it cost you to close your eyes . . .
and see home?
Because all I is is a Black man in America.
Sometimes that seems the hardest.
Till I realized in order to survive . . .
I have to close my eyes and see that—
Home is Where The Heart Is . . .
My freedom, my freedom.
MY FREEDOM!
PEACE.

Father Time

PEACE.
I loved him then—
His skin was black as day light,
his voice was like a P.A. system for the world.
When he spoke,
we listened.
He was alive.
He tried to buy me everything,
as if everything was for sale.
Funny thing?
He couldn't buy more time with me.
They say "it heals all wounds,"
but time is also a snitch,
because it tells me of his negligence,
a ghost I knew of.
I never understood,
so I guess I never really knew.
Love him?—
His skin is black as night light,
folding into itself.
His voice fades before the words ever hit the wind,
with letters not legible.
No one listens.
Now he's dying.
He did buy me one precious thing,
as if this thing wasn't precious:
Forgiveness.
Sad thing?
I never used enough time to give it to him,
but time did heal me.
How much I still love him—
my father time.
PEACE.

CHEY-PATRON

Mysterious Shadow

There's a groundhog inside of me that wants to come out, but every time he sees his shadow he hides. That's no doubt. This shadow has chased him his whole life, and he could never figure out why. Maybe he's being chased by his past and all his unpleasant experiences, so when his shadow appears, he tends to hide in his own internal chasm. Deep down in his soul, this is all he knows. Little does he know that all he has to do is try to bring his shadow into the sunlight. Once he establishes this, he'll realize the sunlight is a symbol of love that can overpower any shadow that's been chasing him throughout his life.

Life on the Road

Life is like a vehicle on a long road. You can decide which paths to take. In these paths of life, there are obstacles that can slow down your journey to success. Like speed bumps and potholes slowing down the vehicle, there are distractions in life like drugs, negative people, prison, etc. In life, with age comes wisdom. The more you age, the more you're able to distinguish right from left, when to stop and go, just like an expert driver naturally knows the right short cuts to get to a destination the safest way possible. All in all, this is the righteous path we should all follow. *You choose.*

My Legacy

Sometimes I sit and wonder
Where I would be today
Had I made different choices,
Changed my path along the way.

Could I have mastered greatness,
Had a lifetime full of bliss?
The memories I could've had,
And which important ones did I miss?

But when I see your face,
A reflection of my life rises.
You give me the energy I need
To elevate and succeed.

Without you, my life would've remained tumultuous.
All the anger would've enveloped me.
You are my remedy.
For you, my loving son,
Are my masterpiece
I'll leave behind for many years to come.
The greatness that I longed for
At last I did achieve.

Hope You Notice My Endeavors

Going out of your way means selflessness, an overflowing love expecting nothing in return, not for your own satisfaction, but for theirs.

Personally, I went out of my way many times in response to people's wishes. This time in particular is different because it meant commitment even when I wasn't prepared. I was young—eleven, to be exact. That still doesn't give me the right to turn my back on you, for you to become a bastard and I a coward. So I didn't, and I stuck in there, putting my selfish ways to the side, like when Christmas came around and all the presents shifted to you.

I know I left you when you were five. One thing for certain, I tried. So maybe in the future, once you're a grown man, you can learn not to resent me for all the lost times. Instead, go against the grain and go out of your way to forgive me, showing me what it means to have an overflowing love, expecting nothing in return.

Untitled

I would rather live life abundantly,
but it's not that simple.
Earn credentials and at least become
someone who's influential.
I had the potential but
I didn't take life as an essential.
I would rather travel overseas
and become a boss,
head of my own embassy,
watch my son grow up and
live through my legacy.

I would rather stay loyal
until I'm under the soil
and beyond mortality
than to be a man without purpose
and a cloudy moral compass.
Make accurate choices
and channel my emotions
with positive energy.
Give a thoughtful effort to
continue to optimize
my state of mind and body.
Then, maybe,
just maybe,
the "I would rather's"
will turn into my casual reality.

ISRAEL

The Fawn

I was born on a farm in southeastern Ohio, near the Ohio River, in the woods, in a pile of falling leaves under and near a bunch of beech trees that surrounded me and my mother on the top of a hill near a meadow.

It was the dead of night in the winter as I lay there shivering and afraid of this new world. I looked up and saw and felt my mother licking me, and as I looked above her through the branches on these majestic trees, I saw a thousand stars in the black velvet night twinkling above me as if to say "Hello," and at that moment all my fears and chills went away as I felt safe and loved and slowly drifted off to sleep.

When I awoke the next morning, I could feel the cold air being kept from me by the warmth of my mother's body, so I felt the courage to try to stand while staying near her. Soon as I started to lift myself, I could feel my legs tremble as if they did not know what to do, and as quick as I stood was as quick as I fell on the frozen crunchy leaves, all the while my mother watching with a loving smile.

So, with that smile I felt the courage to try again, but this time Mother helped to lift me to my hooves with her soft snout under my chest and front legs for support, and with that I was even more encouraged to stand as the cold brisk air enveloped my warm but weak body.

There I was, scared and excited as I stood upon these trembling legs along with my mother's support and love, and so I tried to jump for joy as the sun rose over the hill and shined upon my face as if to say, "You can do it!," and I did, but my landing was awful, yet I was so proud of myself.

257

My mother stood up on her legs, tall and graceful she was as she walked toward me to nudge me with her nose and lie down beside me, and at that I felt safe and comforted as I lay near her brown fur and nursed upon her breasts until I slowly drifted off to sleep.

My life as a young fawn taught me to enjoy all of nature. The smells of fresh winter bark, the voice that I heard as the wind blew through the trees, the comfort of the warm sun as I grazed through the meadow, and the sky that came to life at night as stars flew across the darkness above. But most of all was my mother's unconditional love and protection as I grew. I am the person I am today all because of the life I once knew.

Lessons

This is what I've
learned with gifts
painfully earned

        Life is like the face of
        a raging river that
        glistens in the shower
        of the sun where it is
        warm but in its depth
        is ice cold darkness

Like a spruce so young
surrounded by giants
keeping from it the creator's
love and nutrients to make it strong

        Yet through all this
        I know
        the river calms
        into a shallow pool
        where all is warm
        and glistening

And the giants
burn or timber
so the young spruce
receives the creator's love

The Inner Man

You'll feel abandoned,
yes, all alone,
like a youngling with
a mother moose, soon
to have a newborn.

You'll know not why,
no matter how much
it hurts, but off
you must go to wander
this earth.
You'll not forget,
no, you never will,
but in time this will heal.

Threats and danger
wherever you go,
hungry wolves to
chase you so.

Listen, though, as you roam,
for He is calling to lead
you home.
Hear His voice as
it whispers through
the trees, by a subtle
wind, a subtle breeze.

Look to the sky,
look to the sun
as it warms your face,
as it sits on a throne.

Lie down and rest,
graze and feed,

He will provide
all you need.
        Trust in him,
        this I know,
                I promise you,
                youngling, His love
                will never go.

STYLUS

I Am Whoo I Am

You see
    a donkey because
    I want you to see a donkey.
You see
    a weak spot because
    I want you to see a weak spot.
You see
    an easy victory because
    I want you to see an easy victory.

But I see everything!

You see,
    the truth lies in the eyes;
    therefore, you must look deep.
You see,
    some wear their hearts on their sleeves,
    while most have it concealed.
You see,
    the truth lies beneath the surface,
    so most find it difficult to find.
You see,
    most have a manipulative motive,
    while some just seek genuine companionship.

But I see everything!

You see
    a donkey because,
    by portraying the jackass,
    it is much clearer
    for the owl inside of me
    to filter
    the snakes in the grass,
    sharks in the water,
    and rats in the sewer!
You see,
    real recognizes real,
    and real eyes realize real lies!

Life's Highway

Life is like a highway,
its temptations disguised as exits
distracting us from reaching our destination.
I'm guilty of
exiting in the "Hartbeat"
to make it rain at the Gold Club.

I'm guilty of
exiting at the "Elm"
to see them boys down bottom.
I'm guilty of
exiting onto the reservation
to shoot some dice at the 'wood.

Now I have learned that,
even though there's always an entrance ramp
to get back onto Life's Highway,
there comes a point where we realize that
we have limited gas left in our tanks.
And in order to achieve our goals,
tunnel vision,
cruise control, and
staying in our lanes are
the keys to avoiding those gas-burning city miles.

Untitled

You can't have it all—
My future, my freedom.
To think I'd go back,
I can't be that dumb.

The harder you work on me,
The harder I work on you.
The difference, though,
Is I know your next move.

The relationships you've broken—
My family, my friends—
The bridges you've burned
That I now must mend.

The odds are with you,
Numbers don't lie.
As I watch the bodies drop,
I salute and say bye.

VERONICA-MAY CLARK

Transient Random Noisebursts with Accompaniment

There you are in front of me
You do not see me I see you
You are not me I see you do not see me

I see my eyes I see you dress my face
I address your face
I put you in my dress and there you are not me

I cannot fit inside your box
I am misshaped
I do not fit I am misshaped
My box is not for you
I want to fit inside my box
But there you do not fit
Your box is different than my box
You cannot fit in mine
I want to go inside my box
There is no box for me
I look for boxes for myself
But there are none for me

To live outside for you is death to me
To live the life of death in someone living
To know the pain I know you do not know
Impossibly I wait not me
To throw you on the surgeon's knife to live
To live outside for me is death to you
To know you do not know the pain I know

Impossibly I wait not you

Impossibility of life inside the death of someone living
    of living life outside of someone dying
Impossibility of life outside the death of someone living
    a living death inside a life of dying

Your reflections face my eyes I only see
I have never seen me only you
You are you do not ask I do not know you
This is how it is for me not you

I cannot see me see I cannot see me
I cannot bear to look I cannot see
Please do not look at you I cannot see me
I cannot see me see I cannot see

Still Life with a Hook, Wall, Bra, and Fan

On a hook, fixed to a concrete wall,
Suspends a tiny bra, gently held,
Enveloped by a nearby fan's sweet
Whispering, drying sinusoidally,
Like a hummingbird's wings in slow motion.
Its diaphanous and delicate white
Skin showers kisses over the cold wall,
As if to wake a lover just departed.

We Can

We can confuse intelligence with fear
We can praise the Lord in many ways
We can go about our business
We can live life well or poorly
We can be ourselves and play pretend
We can stay and help and run and hide
We can go along because we're afraid
We can rail loudly of injustice against our group
We can silently whisper hatred toward another
We can act rationally
We can rationalize ourselves away
We can debate openly and honestly without anger
We can quash opposition by force
We can love the multitude of differences in others
We can tolerate intolerance and allow fear to win the day
We can redefine bigotry to rationalize our own
We can prefer to use the word "faith" because the word "hope" scares us
We can surround ourselves with others like ourselves and pretend
the world away
We can repeat the things that bear repeating
We can repeat the things that bear repeating
We can respectfully challenge our elders
We can rewrite the dictionary to rationalize our hypocrisy
We can blame institutions broadly without context
We can be blind to our common ground
We can see the good inside us all
We can feel oppressed even by people oppressed
We can pretend everything is OK
We can love and be loved
We can load our guns for battle in order to feel safe

We can meet in the middle then go our separate ways
We can pretend the synchronized nodding of heads is proof of truth
We can think or delegate this responsibility
We can pretend that all of this is OK
We can wonder why we're here and pretend we really know
We can feel the pain of exclusion and then also exclude
We can pretend the only way to stand for something is through physical force
We can stand for peace and love for all
We can never understand the other and therefore know it all
We can know that pain is universal but so are love and hope
We can hear truth spoken, understand, but fear affirming out loud because our group
membership is at stake
We can even pretend that Black lives don't matter and
We can also pretend that transgender girls chose to be that way
We can choose open and honest dialogue
We can say the things that people think but are afraid to say
We can hear the furtive murmuring in amongst the crowd
We can leave uncomfortable silence in our wake

Bad Brains

It's very dark.
She's driving home again
after a hard day riding the mountain.
It's late enough to be early.

She looks as she passes:
an oversize pickup
idling in the commuter lot
just off the highway,
lights all ablaze.

Driving on,
thinking: ominous looking truck.

Right at the light,
past the Misty Vale,
the long straight stretch of road
disappearing into the trees and hills,
and just before she climbs,
there, far behind her in the distance,
the lights of the pickup
appear a moment before she climbs into the hills.

Up and turning as she climbs,
her little Rabbit GTI
singing softly into the night,
the road bending left then right
then left again
where the roadbuilders blasted through,
the rock walls pressed right up against the road

of the hairpin turn.
She knows the road well
and slows to thirty-five
to navigate safely through the rocky pass in the dark of night.

But then, suddenly,
the heavens open up behind her,
a blinding white light
and the sound of crunching metal,
smashing glass,
and a sudden thrust of speed
lifting her into the other lane
and up the steep embankment
just before the cliffs,
and then flipping back into the road
landing upside down,
glass shards scattering all around her,
and she hears the sound of the truck's roar,
its tires screeching closely past her head,
her eyes wide in amazement,
seeing the wheels fly by in the night.

Then silence
and the cold night air,
suspended there
upside down,
held in place by her seat belt,
searching for its clasp,
tumbling head over heels
onto the ceiling covered in glass.

Crawling out, her hands bleeding,
shaken and stunned,
not yet fully grasping what has just occurred.

A car stops.
A figure.
"Whoa! Are you all right?" calls a voice in the night.
"That guy just ran you off the road!"
"Yeah," she says.

They stand together in the cold dark night next to
the crumpled wreck
in the middle of the road on its back
while someone runs to a nearby house
to call for help.
And then again, the voice in the dark:
"Hey, did you go to Newtown?"
"Yeah," she says, still shaking. "I graduated in '94."

In Relegation

A window hides the night sky
A clock lies on the shelf
A chair made of plastic stands in the corner and cries

A rug lies dead on the floor

Junk food together with friends feels lonely
The ceiling separates the angry walls
Porcelain basks in the dark

A hot pot burns with desire

There's a gender non-conforming spoon/fork combo
The bunk is afraid to admit she's an anvil
Marks on the wall tell only those who know

The cell objectifies

There's a pile of books forced into a life of hard labor
The T.V. constructs a new light saber
The door begs forgiveness for all it's done

The blue pencil's mad that the green team has won

Three Haiku

A tree holds ground
On top of the mountain
Mangled, scarred, windblown

Observe guards and men
Watching each other
Without looking

Flowers grow inside
Just as well if shown the same
Love and kindness

Searching for Contour by Veronica May-Clark

Song of Herself

I am the song that I sing and the wind in my hair
I love bluebird mountain mornings
I am a butterfly floating through time
I used to skate every single day

I am the song that I sing and the wind in my hair
I go here and there all alone
I wait for the good things on their way to arrive
I work on my faults every day

I am the song that I sing and the wind in my hair
My favorite nail polish is blue
I love threading daisies into a chain
And I hear dots and loops in my mind

I am the song that I sing and the wind in my hair
And can cry and be scared and know love
Where I'm from, there are hills made of green
Left a boy, I return wearing heels

I am from a place in Scotland named
Motherwell

Untitled

My clothing is taken,
only my underwear allowed to remain,
legs bare, no socks at all,
torso naked, arms freezing.
Only a suit made of white transparent paper—
all I'm allowed
one November.
Hands freezing, every step shooting daggers
up into my shins and knees through my bare heels,
hammered in by concrete made of ice.
November November November November.
Wrists clad in cold, lifeless steel,
chained to the one ahead, the one behind,
everyone else bundled up—jackets, sweaters, boots—
everyone else watching me, dumbstruck,
shackles painfully secured about my ankles.
Loaded up into the ice cream truck,
the filthy floor, my feet on the filthy floor, freezing.
Back out into the sally port,
back out onto ice—same as the truck, same as before,
The courthouse floor, waiting to enter
into the bullpen along with fifty others,
standing, freezing, numb,
ankles aching, metal banging bones,
paraded,
forced into the courtroom through a door at the front,
theatrically positioned there at the front,
hundreds of people, all aghast,
the pure spectacle of it all.
An attorney appears,

whispering something, clearly shocked,
bailiffs laughing, pointing at my feet, bare,
my underwear clearly visible through
the diaphanous white paper that might as well not exist.
November November November November.
Dragging roughly out and away at almost a run,
the metal shackles hammering my bones.
So cold, so cold.
Now another chain,
wrapped about my torso so tightly
it's difficult to breathe.
So cold.
Alone now waiting inside a solitary cell.
So cold
So cold
So very, very cold.

In Memory of My Mother

Praise to my mum and praise to my dad
    And praise to the sister that I never had
Praise to my brother who's always been there
    And praise to the girl with the bow in her hair
Praise to the daisies who seem to exist
    To anchor the dew of mid-morning mist
Praise to the flowers and praise to the grass
    And praise to the showers in sun from the past
Praise to the children whose parents adore
    And praise to the garden in winter and war
Praise to myself and also to you
    For God only knows what we're here to do
A note to sustain however my song
    And praise to us all even after we're gone.

JOHN-RUSSELL BOSSÉ

True Story: Petr

I learned how to play chess in my freshman year at Lynn English High, 1991. It was during a library study period, to be exact. I was fifteen.

I couldn't get enough of it and played everybody I could. Not all, though, were eager to indulge my enthusiasm, and most were reluctant to clash with me in my new hobby. Out of the many acquaintances I made at that time, however, there was only one that I needed to play.

I met Petr in our school's chess club. He was a junior and part of the chess team, which I promptly joined. Petr was meek and quiet, with a dry sense of humor and a cool confidence over the board. He was at least six feet tall, skinny, and thickly bespeckled with a pale greasy complexion—not popular with the girls, but neither was I. His family was poor and had recently immigrated from Russia, probably to escape persecution, since they were Jews.

His mother, Mrs. Pashkov, was a round, jolly woman, maybe one of the kindest people I have ever met. She would always welcome me into their downtown apartment with such joy and open arms, like I was a long-lost son. Even though they didn't have much, she was generous, insisting I eat, and so I would eat like them. They taught me the wonders of cream cheese and lox with eggs and bagels; taught me some Russian words; and showed me that I was no match in chess for anyone in their family.

Petr's father, Vladimir, played postal chess. He was a wiry, quiet, gray-haired man in his fifties or sixties. His English was almost non-existent. In the little he did know, however, he'd often labor to exhort that I must study, study, study to become a good chess player—that I would never become a good player otherwise. He would stand over some of my games with Petr with an air of good-humored disapproval, because I still had much to learn in the language of chess.

Petr's pretty sister Alla was probably three or four years his senior. I was no match for her either.

Unbeknownst to me, we were living in the wake of the Bobby Fischer craze and in the midst of both Polgar Sister-mania and the post-Cold War chess migration. It was in these heady days, in 1991, that Petr and I would play every day after school and visit different chess clubs on certain evenings during the week.

I remember the older men in some clubs who were stuck with having to play me, a fifteen-year-old neophyte. With leisure and a lazy hand, they would read newspapers and cast around dull eyes for anyone who could actually challenge them—while defeating me as an afterthought. If I were to, though, now say, "Fuck you too," it would be said with the utmost humor and affection.

Petr's family gave me unlimited access to their large library of old chess books. Since they were all in Russian, I couldn't read the instruction or commentary, but Petr taught me how to read the algebraic chess notations that recorded each game. That was my first exposure to "Legal's Mate" and where I tried, in vain, to decipher the usefulness of what I would later learn was a "fianchetto."

I remember how, one day, Petr's (Russian?) friend Sasha broke off from speaking to Petr to ask me about one of the English meanings of Petr's name. Though they were speaking in Russian, I sensed some disagreement between the two on this matter. Though I was trying to play Petr in a game, Sasha urged me to confirm one of the more humorous interpretations of his friend's name. He laughed when I finally conceded that "Peter" was another name for penis. I hope Petr didn't have any money riding on that debate.

I remember how I would unwittingly torture my friend. I would take so long to make such bad moves that he eventually introduced his Russian-made chess clock to speed me up. After my flag dropped, though, I would often refuse to fully accept defeat and play on, to his frustration.

We might have played a total of over 200 games, and maybe I won four. In high school, though, I never let him forget those wins into which I stumbled. When I beat him for the first time, I ran to his mother to tell her. She was so joyous and effusive in her congratulations that I imagined her wanting to adopt me. Her praise was like a glorious shower to wash away all my defeats.

My stints in a psych hospital and state adolescent mental health treatment programs interrupted further matchups between us until Petr and I met again on the internet as adults. We also met over the board when I was about twenty-three. I managed to beat him once or twice in the maybe thirteen games of those last meetings.

I laud him for his patient tolerance and willingness to play such an inferior opponent so many times. Since the age of fifteen I have wistfully compared my level of play with his and have pushed myself to do better.

Petr is like a lighthouse on a distant shore. Through life's nightgales and storms, he has been a driver of self-improvement and advancement, because my goal has been to, one day, become at least as good as he was.

I wonder if knowing, admiring, and clashing with him in those gracious moments also drove me to become a better person in other areas of life. Maybe chess was a starting point from which my confidence could expand elsewhere.

I try to live like he did—or how I observed him through those brief windows of our society. Life was good to us, and it allowed us to become better and to strive toward even more promising shores.

If I could take away one thing from my friendship with Petr, it would be this: the acquired drive to work toward one day being like him, a lighthouse and exemplar.

My Cry to the Naked

If we continue to look away
from the spying NSA—
being cattle who hold not
their government at bay;

If we accept the label of "extreme"
for all those who keep the dream
of individual freedoms and self-esteem;

If we suppress our "Why's" and swallow the lies
and refuse to rise to the watchman's cries;

If we sleep soundly and reject roundly
that the state's senses are around thee,
and in our bedrooms are their ears,
in violation of whom we hold near—
our intimate murmurings for them to hear;

If we leave our dignity in the dust;
If we sacrifice our liberty on the altar of trust;
If we glibly claim we have "nothing to hide,"
or our fears and doubts we elide,

Then we'll be naked and vulnerable—along for the ride—
exposed to the laws they will make on their side.

Gather a council against the panopticon.
Shore up your rights before they are gone.
Boycott and agitate while there's still time.
Make your voice heard before it's a crime!

Our Mistress and Demigods

Ancient utterances laced through amply-filled silken bodices: Poetry should thus bind us over a mysterious and perennial heart.

She should be captured with our mouths even past midnight, when her charms may ignite our minds.

Her many layers of meaning should dip pen and soul in the feverish desire to reveal —

Reveal the soft, naked valleys and crests that describe her.

And from this fount of inspiration, as elusive as smoke in our hands, may we form her blazing lines —

Lines we will burn with, to brand eons into pages borne like demigods throughout the ages.

Some Writing Prompts For Those Who Have No Difficulty Imagining Them

Write about justice deferred or withheld.

Write about being convicted of something you didn't do.

Write about pretrial confinement or years of isolation that make you want to rip out your eyes.

Write about the little voice inside you that speaks from a stilled heart while you pace breaths in a

place quieter than death. Let that voice speak secrets that liberate beyond any bondage imposed upon the flesh.

Write about routine so entrenched that, if you needed to, you could navigate the day blind.

Write about apathy.

Write about a world in which no one believes you.

Write about wanting to give up.

Write about the composure of a jury who enjoyed the unflinching belief that they had executed

Justice, and then write about the concurring triumph of a sentencing judge or the satisfaction of his gavel.

Write about how something can be lodged in your memory like a splinter of steel.

Write about the aging years of death row solitary.

Write about pleading for your life to deaf ears.

Write about the last twenty yards you'll ever walk.

Write about the feel of leather straps.

Write about staring down the barrels of executioner's needles.

Write about the refuge of your inner voice.

Write about wanting to go home.

KEITH ELLIS

Mania

Mania makes me feel alive, like the sun in the sky.
Mania makes me feel like a champion, like Tom Brady in the pocket.
Mania gives people the desire to marry me.
Mania gives people the desire to murder me.
Mania makes me creative, like a songwriter in Nashville.
Mania gets me high, like a junky in the alley.
Mania makes me treat sleep like the plague.
Mania makes me treat food like a prostate exam.
Mania makes me treat people like robots or trees.
Mania makes me treat the world around me like a dream.
Mania makes me laugh, mania makes me smile.
Mania makes me do backflips inside.
Mania makes me sensitive to negative energy.
Mania makes me see the lemonade instead of lemons.
Mania makes me aware.
Mania forces me to pay attention.
Mania makes me productive.
Mania makes me destructive.
Mania and lithium had a love child.
Hypo-mania is born.
Hypo-mania is me.
I don't ever want to change
positive energy and finding a way to win.
To be depressed is the equivalent of death,
quite literally, for people who know what true mania is.
The opposite of mania is death.
I'll take my chances.
I'll take my lithium.
I'll be hypo-manic.
I will be happy.

Outside Looking In

I choose to write outside of the margins of my paper. I do not believe this to be a "bad" habit, necessarily, but I do make a conscious decision not to stay "within the borders." Perhaps I have a problem following rules (so I've been told), but I think it would be more accurate to say I have a problem with following rules that don't make sense. I just don't buy into the idea, for example, that a paper company encourage the consumer to use paper in a less than efficient way—to increase their sales. Call me crazy, I just don't feel like going on forever like a sucker, like I've been had. I don't stay within the border because I don't pay sticker price at the dealership, I don't pay for extra mayo on my Whopper at Burger King or extra tartar sauce for my Fish Fillet at McDonald's—because it doesn't make sense. I don't buy into the notion that, because I'm tall, I should be great at basketball—I stink—or, because I grew up poor in Waterbury, that I should die poor in Waterbury. I use my whole slice of paper because every conversation is an opportunity to profit intellectually, because every lemon can become lemonade, and every negative reframed into a positive. I don't stay within the border because I have a hunger for more. I use way too much garlic powder and red pepper flakes on my pizza. I take a long time to say "When" while the pretty waitress at Olive Garden sprinkles parmesan cheese on my soup or pasta. I use more laundry powder than the packet instructs. I don't follow the speed limit when I know I can get away with it. I tuck my tee shirt into my sweatpants in prison. In prison, I live with a trans-gender woman. I tint the windows on my cars. I believe in governing yourself and not relying on the approval or permission of other people. I do not follow rules that don't make sense, like staying in the border, because by breaking them and thinking independently, I feel powerful. Feeling powerful is a powerful feeling—not power over anyone or anything, but power over my own fate. I have absolute control over what happens to me—good or bad. By following my own rules, I can accept the consequences. Not writing inside the lines, this habit of mine, will enable me to win at the highest level.

If

If your mind is the master, then you should think like a winner.
If it's always about the money all the time, then manage your pennies, because it's the small money that matters.
If winners win, then winning is a lifestyle.
If network equals net worth, then network with people who know what it means to win.
If power is more important and more valuable than society's opinion, then win strength and influence by studying the masses.
If integrity is the cornerstone of greatness, then make your actions honorable, your thoughts wholesome, and your spoken word true.
If goodness is the greatest, then be good! Good people do good things, and good things happen to good people.
If you can build by adding on, then build with bricks and cement, or with wisdom and understanding. Contribute to the collective energy of perfection by maintaining an optimistic outlook on life and sharing it with others.
If we are all born winners, then start any time to think like an infant. Everything in the world will be new and wonderful once you break free from the chains of influence that society has on your thinking.
If you can do it once, then do it ten times. Ten dimes is a dollar. Remember, any situation can always be ten times worse. However, by thinking positive, or thinking like a winner, every situation can be ten times better. Strive for the best.
If your will is parallel to the will of the universe, then your will is the will of God. When God said, "Let there be light," there was light. So, when Man has found the light, his wildest dreams will manifest into reality.

MICHAEL P. MARK, JR.

Inside of Me

lost in thought the world disappeared before my eyes
finally tranquility no more lies no one dies
as my heart aches my spirit cries out
but no one hears me I'm all alone
I search and I search but I can't find home
when will I know what I'm searching for
I left the seed that grew at two
the pain I feel if you only knew
    will I ever feel again
behind the mask is pain and sorrow
I live today to die tomorrow
but how can I forget about yesterday
green fields clear skies blue oceans
my peace of mind
my life
explosions
the pieces to the puzzle seem to never fit
what is a life lived without love
what is the rainbow without the dove
THERE'S STILL SOMETHING MISSING

I Would Rather

I would rather be myself than be
what others want me to be.
I would rather be respected than accepted,
because to me being accepted doesn't mean
that you're being respected.
You see, they would rather accept you
for who they want you to be
than to respect you for who you are.
I would rather be in control of my emotions
than allow someone else to control them for me.
I would rather not give you the power.
I would rather be than to never have been . . .
But to never be is to never have been.

Hopeless Romantic

You were on my mind today
We're so close yet so far away
I never thought it would end up like this
All I can do is sit back and reminisce
I've held onto all our memories
Sometimes I wonder if you ever think of me
They say it's better to have loved and lost
than to have never loved at all
But here I stand
I've loved and I've lost
I try to stand but yet I fall
I still don't know if it's okay or not for me to cry
But every day without your love
a piece of me dies

My Life Was

My life was
    turned around
        and spun
upside down
    as if it was
a tornado   that
    hit me
        swiftly . . .

                         I

lost

                   my
way
I   can   only

                     hope

to   find
the

                   path

    today

JOHN L. BENJAMIN

If

If, if, if . . .
If I knew better, I'd do better.
If I did better, I'd see less failure.
If failure is disappointment, I got a lot of people shaking their heads.
If that didn't happen, then what?
If he or she had been there, then what would of happened?
If, if, if . . .
There it goes again.
If you keep doing the same thing that you have always done, you
going to get the same thing that you
    always gotten.
If you keep getting the same thing you always got, what do you have?
If you don't have nothing to show for it, I'd say nothing.
If . . .
If is a word of choice, like Or.
If shows uncertainty.
If is life without two letters.
If, if, if.

One For the Team

You can call me the quarterback, because when
I see you I'm not running back.
I call the play but when I seen the defense, audibly:
hot route, kill kill.
You know what, time out.
I'm one of the best at this game, like Derek Jeter,
even though you threw me a curve ball I
treated it like a change up, because when I hit that
grand slam, I changed up.
I had home field advantage, and you came into my
octagon and made me submit.
What I'm getting at is taking one for the team.
You know, doing something you may not condone but
someone could benefit from it.
Now you may not approve but I benefitted
from it,
I enjoyed it,
I took time out my way for it, it's just I took no time
getting rid of it.
The things I do.

Son of a P.K.

No Dru Hill, just Cisco; no Rick Ross, just Rose; and
no Remy Martin just . . . well, Remy Martin.
You see, I should of seen it when he was younger
he never was interested in St. Nick but always took
notice of St. Ives.
I never thought nothing of it though, not until he cheated
on his girlfriend Alize with Tanqueray.
But I didn't intervene, not even when he started
bringing his friends to the house.
There's these twins called E & J, but I call them Evil
Juice, cause every time he hangs out with them it's like
he's another person and his dark side comes out.
And then you got Jack Daniels, Samuel Adams, and
don't even get me started on Jim Beam.
But I can't control who he's friends with.
So what is it?
When he was younger, we were not only a family but
I also taught him we're a team.
I don't know why but he wanted our mascot to be
a grey goose and represent Amsterdam even though
we lived in Bel Air.
That was weird.
One thing I did try to do was to always have
some father-son time,
So, one day I taught him Poker . . . that failed.
Every time he has a boat he'll call Capt. Morgan, four
of a kind, four Loko, and if he has an Ace of Spades
he's going all in!
I just don't get it
I used to be his hero, now he turns to the Incredible
Hulk,
Doesn't wear Louis Vuitton no more, just Louis 13.
He doesn't even come home anymore, but when I look
in that mirror across the bar, I know he'll be there.

HUNTER McGINTY

A Deer in the Yard

                The
        grass is greener
on the other side.
        Eating dandelions   and
                weeds, chickadees looking for seeds. A perfect place
                to relieve myself. On the hill is a trove of butterfly
                bushes, tempting but in clear sight of danger. Some
                times they come unexpectedly, like illegal immigrants.
                We are not welcome in their country. They will
            unleash their   guardians,   who chase us
            back in to the   foliage. But   we are not
            the only un-   welcome   guests.
            We've heard   from   squirrels,

                    chipmunks, mice,
                snakes, opossums about
                this all-you-can-eat buffet.
                The forest is barren. We
                    scrounge most
                    meals. Some
                        overseers
                have   pity   on us.
                They watch from their watchtowers.
                    I've had my picture taken. I'm
probably on their neighborhood watch list. Our coexistence is an
anomaly. We trespass by nature, but who is to say that we are not
equal in ownership? My purpose is to wander; theirs is to occupy and
protect. If I am caught in their crosshairs, I run. But their fortresses
will be swarmed again. Who's to say I'm not welcome when it's
practically being given away?

Morning Accountability Plan

The door pops.
Another day.
You don't want to do this.
You don't want to think about the time.
Coffee and oatmeal, no surprises.
You keep seeing people come in and out.
It makes you depressed.
You won't get a second chance.
You think back to how it used to be
when you got up early and had responsibilities.
But your hands were not clean,
the secrets you could not hide.
Handcuffs and shame,
the things that saved your life.
How will you face those people?
That can come later.
The forgiveness of God is not new to this stranger.
Future ambitions?
You'll take what you can get.
Felonies and misdemeanors society won't forget.
You're on your own journey.
Don't give up hope.
The sun is still shining.
You're not alone.
There's still a world out there.
Take this time to think, like:
Don't sweat the little things.
Focus on what's important.
It could always be worse.
Be thankful for what you have.

We're all in this together.
This world isn't so dark if you can think in this way.
Suddenly being arrested seems to fade away.
There's still good you can do, please don't forget.
Every morning is a gift, cherish it.
What can you give not what can you get.
Don't go through life with regrets.

This Rotten Thing

Anger will not serve me well going forward. It's something that I've just been keeping to myself. I've allowed this seed to grow into a strong tree without properly understanding how to care for it. Its roots are a part of me, so I can't pull it out. I need my STIHL chainsaw to cut away my anger at its heels. I want to understand why this always gets out of hand.

First, I cut away the branches of jealousy. Acceptance is the oil to my chain. I cut through the middle of revenge. The sap oozes tears and regret. I roll each piece through medication, therapy, and church, but only the bark comes off. I lift the closest piece, the time that I yelled at my celly, onto the red wood splitter. An apology and a helping hand easily separate this piece. I dig deeper through my pile and find that painful fight with my dad. Filled with knots and bitter words my machine will strain against this mass. But your love for me is greater and crushes that ugly mess.

I split a lot of turmoil and fear in there as well. I see now that there are many things that make up this angry tree. At its core is friction to a much more powerful force. No matter what I do, this tree will sprout again. But as I sit in prison, self-control has become my friend. Never again will I allow my anger to grow into this rotten thing.

KAREEM LEACH

Namiko

Child of the waves:
swaying to and fro, thrashing and crashing,
moving and swelling, banging and smashing.
Child of the waves:
those who've surfed me, I've drowned,
swallowed them up to push them to the depths
to never be found.
Child of the waves:
whether hello or goodbye,
whether a ten-fingered gesture
or one of just five.
Child of the waves:
finger wave, swelling wave, light wave,
crime wave, sound wave, down wave,
short waves, long waves, wavelengths, all waves.
Child of the waves:
I have taken many forms,
never swayed by convention or by society's norms.
My father's a tsunami, my mother a storm.
Child of the waves:
I was birthed, I was born
Child of the Waves.

JENKINS TARLUE

Longed Nemesis

We are ants,
Stuck in a very dark place.
In and out these walls we creep,
Our steps are without a beat.
Our strength is three-fold our weight,
Stronger than the two-legged,
But still to them we are of no weight.
But behind these walls,
Behind these walls we have a fighting chance.
Our six small legs only run so fast,
The energy of the two-legged is short-lasted,
With stress, hidden tears, and depression they are crippled,
With our escapes sometimes we giggle.
In similarity of us and the longed enemy,
We all run
From pain, addiction, lust, fantasy, fear, and envy.
They run, and from them we run.
What are we—
We are ants creeping through the little holes of the prison walls.

Internal Prison Cell

Desired are the exuberant moments in life,
The smiles, search for self, and gratitude,
The stress-free freedom to live and love.
But what happens when men and women are placed in restraints,
Nonphysical, but mental, restraints—
Fear of love, chance, risk,
Worries of work, children, school,
Scared by the media, TV news, internet,
All examples of some of the many mental restraints,
Some caused by the extrovert, others by introvert forces?
Internal death exists within the ones among us
Who have been stripped of their desires, love, and inner happiness.
Binkies are given to those who fail to act,
Those who allow themselves to remain tied down,
Virtual to the true self,
As darkness remains on the hidden.
Light shines on those who seek it.

BRYAN GOODWIN

Gangsters' Paradise

They call it Paradise. I call it just a dream,
Because there is no Paradise for gangsters
Who are naïve.
The omen put it in our minds just so he could see
If we would follow in his steps and hurt our enemies.
He wants to take out our souls and keep them eternally
And use us as a puppet to fulfill his evil deeds.
So, if that is a Gangsters' Paradise, it sounds like hell to me,
A place where you will spend your life in pain and misery.

Born in the Cold

Born in the cold
Just hours old
Found in the cold
All alone in the cold
Babyboy crying in the cold
Tears frozen on my face
Face frozen from the cold
Now 38 years later
I've survived the cold

Untitled

I am a man with a dream
Not a man in a dream
As I wake and reality sets in
Why am I here?
Growing up was rough at times
But I managed because
I am a man with a dream

I am a man with a dream
Stubborn at times, most will say
Never backing down. I wonder
Will I ever listen to what others have to say?
That I am a man with a dream

I am a man with a dream
And I plan to follow my dream
That is to find my birth parents
But, after all, I am a man with a dream
I am from Bridgeport, CT

A Dog's Life

Sometimes I'm the meanest
Sometimes I'm the nicest.
Raised in a good home,
Roaming around
Till
The guy
Found me
A new home.
Walked to my
Cell, hearing
Barks like mine.
Around my neck,
Leashes and chains
Which they are not
Made for walking,
As I'm placed in my
new home with a
bowl and slop, just like
my old home, waiting for
someone to come find me to
take me back home. As night
falls, I cry   myself to
Sleep. This   is a dog's life
Inside   a pound.

TALL EAGLE

Oyata Tatanka

Often I think of you
In my thoughts and heart
I honor you
Your ancestors' blood stained Mother Earth red
Their bones are forever rooted in her bosom
The voices of your relatives are upon the four winds
With the message of long ago
Hear them
Welcome to the gifted ones
That walk upon the plains today
May you find the best and sweetest of pastures
May you always be remembered
The greatness of your Nation
As one gazes over all your land
In the stories I hear of you of long ago
I give you thanks for your coat
That kept us warm in the long winters
For the covering of our lodges
Thank you for your flesh and bones
For all parts of you, you gave
To improve our lives
May your new generation and those after
Find at last a sanctuary
And live and multiply in peace
May you receive the gift of a long life
May those that look upon you
Remember those before you
And be mournful over the senseless slaughter

Of your brothers and sisters of long ago
May you be free from enemy or predator
May sickness flee from you and evil never come
White Buffalo, we look forward to see you again
White Buffalo, Calf Woman
Thank you for the pipe and the purification lodge
Buffalo Nation, may you walk in beauty
Live in peace and be remembered in love.

POP

Prepare a large canvas of pure white
    place it briefly over the darkness of eternal night
Leaves with many fall colors, not of the summer green
    with an inviting deep blue representing the sky in the scene
Add a mountain off in the far distance
    a gentle breeze blowing without resistance
Calm water flowing someplace nearby
    with a touch of sunshine that's easy on the eyes
Erase your ears and mind of all those troublesome sounds
    add the whippoorwill and songbirds in the background

On the ground there is country bluegrass and honeybees
    the leaves are whispering their secrets from the trees
Follow your nose toward that sweet-smelling air
    breathe deep, comb the snakes from your hair

Place a few butterflies over the land
    have one resting in the palm of your hand
Eyes softly close, taking it all in
    upon your lips rests the slightest grin
Allow yourself to drift within your place of peace
    let the feeling of calmness through your body increase
Carefully, barefooted upon the soft grass stand
    walking slowly upon this blessed land
Enter quietly back into the world you know
    until the next time let your love flow

Remembering the Second First Time

Riding alone in the back of the prison van,
sliding along the steel bench-like seat with every turn,
there are no seat belts to aid me in my attempt
to anchor and secure myself to one spot.
As I gaze out the cage-obstructed back window,
watching the world I once knew
flow out from under me,
leaving me behind with each passing mile,
it's as if my essence is being drained from me.
When I recall that moment, I think how ironic
that my hands and feet are bound in chains
but there is nothing to secure me,
I am at the mercy of the van's movements;
should I tumble and fall upon the filthy floor,
helpless and injured, I would remain
like the forgotten, wadded-up papers on the floor.
It was a beautiful spring day;
the sun was in its fullness,
no clouds to obstruct it,
a clear, bright, beautiful day,
warm and comforting,
the colors outside breathtaking and brilliant.
It was a day meant for lovers
to walk hand in hand.
All I could hear was the rumble of the van
as one long moan of anguish and regret,
and yet I am still mindful of the birds singing.
The air within the van is stale and smells
of old food and musk,
whereas outside, the air is fresh,

the wind uninhibited.
That day, though pleasant,
has become a tormented memory in my prison years.
Those days still come and go as the years pass by,
bringing me to utter sadness and deep inner depression,
knowing that I will never be with or hold
any part of the one girl I will ever love.
Her name is sweet to whisper
and is wonderful music to my ears,
the only thought that is constant in my mind.
From the time I was taken away from her long ago,
not an hour has passed by without thinking of her.
May her name be the first name I breathe out
at the start of each day;
may her name be the last name I utter
with my last breath . . .

JOSEPH GROSSO

I Prepared a Lecture, But This Will Have to Do

Your love of British things rubbed off on me. Now I watch *Victoria* and laugh to myself. When you get mad you breathe fire, but don't ever think that your fire is too hot; it keeps my frost from getting too thick.

I drove us into a snowbank, but when I tried to get out, the wheels just spun in place. By the time I made it out you had already hitch-hiked home. I heard you made it home safe but were exhausted from the trip.

Don't ever let them kid you into thinking you need a chauffeur. You have good instincts and can navigate the old way. Though I'd drive you around, still, if you wanted me too. This time my hands at two and ten. You can recline the seat all the way down or take a nap in the back seat. You know I'd do that if I could.

But I'm stuck in a leaky boat heading south where it can cure my cold . . . if it makes it before I sink. During my voyage I came up with a lot I wanted to tell you. I made charts and graphs and PowerPoints to present it all, but in the end it seemed too much, so I've condensed the important bits here:

—I hope you never need to straighten out your hair
—I hope *Sex and the City* never goes off the air
—I hope you wear my KISS shirt still, but if not, I understand
—I hope that when you drive you still listen to all my bands
—I hope the Little Goose will somehow stay open forever
—I hope you and your mom can reconcile things together
—I hope your taste for bourbon stays with you till the end
—I hope that when you speak you never feel you should pretend

You're like Victoria. Strong queen, vulnerable woman. Perfect equilibrium. That's why I laugh. Don't be afraid to let your fire out once in a while. But if it gets too much for you, just remember: be cool.

Don't Leave Us Alone in the Twilight

A harp stamped with "Made in Heaven"
Rings from your throat.
The sounds are as sweet as the Grand Marnier
You drank by the pint.

I felt satisfied enough to die
In the very moment I heard you sing:
"I never gave it a second thought,
It never crossed my mind,
What's right, what's not,
I ain't the judging kind."

If any soul has heard this and not been moved,
Then a soul they must not have,
For even the angels grew envious
With tears of rage and tears of greed
Over melodies their skill couldn't match.

So they conspired to take you.
They must have cut the brake lines,
Though I'm sure that Grand Marnier didn't help.

However, your resilience stifled their cruel plan,
And so they forfeit their jealous mission,
But irony holds no thing sacred;
He is the painter who views all scenarios
A blank canvas ripe for his palette of pranks.

Indifference is his genre.
The painter cares not for men's struggles,
And so when the angels abandoned their cause
He stroked his brush, revealing a scene
Where you voluntarily submitted.

By way of the motel bathroom
You entered the heavenly gate,
Giving yourself willingly into their care,
Joining the angelic choir,
Adding to heaven's glory.

But heaven doesn't need an augment of glory;
This stolid world would have benefited more.
We need color where it's black and white,
We need song where there's none;
I can vouch for your effectiveness.

Day is fine and night is easy,
But the time in between is hopeless—
Is desperate—is lonesome.
I would have asked, if I was around,
That you not leave us in the twilight.

Cause twilight is the loneliest time of day.

The Color of Death is Blue

The color of death is blue.
I know this 'cause my eyes were less than an inch away,
Our face-velcros stuck together
As I blew to inflate,
But the blueness only intensified.

The color of death is blue.
They aggressively ripped our velcros apart.
They wore blue shirts,
They wore blue pants,
They had blue bags,
His mom came down in blue pajamas.

The color of death is blue.
Round with an embossed M.
Blue on the outside, white in the inside.
Funny, 'cause it makes me
White on the outside and blue in the inside.

Seeing all that color
Made me insane and hungry,
So I ate a bunch of blue footballs.
I woke in a blue room
Wearing blue scrubs
Under blue sheets.

The sound of death is blue
That led me to a common room.
It was the echo of a bruise,
A Black girl in blue scrubs,
Same as mine,
Wrapped in a blue sheet,
Same as mine.

She sang the blues.
She wasn't very pretty.
I loved her for five minutes.
I'll love those five minutes forever.

The color of me is blue.

VAUGHN WALKER (aka LEGEND)

I Came in a Boy, I Will Leave a Man

I came in a boy . . .
Thwarted by insinuations and accusations,
Misguided by elders that survived but failed as a nation!
Hindered by the same mistakes that don't diminish my worth
But only carve out avenues of character in which I search.
I came in a boy, but I will leave a man.

I came in a boy . . .
Bound by loyalty, down for the cause, which was no cause at all!
See . . . Grandma said: when a man fails, it's a man that dusts himself
off, with no help warranted.
So I was blessed with the strength of a woman and the height of a king.
Still . . . when I lost Grandma, I chose the wrong things!!!
I chased dreams with anger,
Threw my worth in the same pot as strangers, and never thought
about the dangers.
I came in a boy, but I will leave a man.

I came in a boy . . .
But I no longer do childish things.
See, I know what childish means;
Only unconditional love can outrun the child in me!
I will bask in the glory of being a poppa to be . . .
Knowing I'll have the opportunity to raise a better me,
Instill wisdom in a better she . . .
Which is pronounced—Queen!
Instead of lashing my seed with the phrase "you better be!"
I came in a boy, but I will leave as a king—you'll see.

A Letter to Mom

Why can't I remember the feel of your love, the warmth of your hug?!
Instead, I'm forced to think about ... what could have been!
Neglectful—I now know that it wasn't mommy's medicine.
Horridly, I remember the pulse of your vein, ink-spots of blood as you
carelessly aim.
Ignorant as a child, thought ... belts noosed around your arm was a
trend, because your waist wasn't as thin.
More than my mom, you were my friend,
The first person I loved, even though you never chose me over drugs
and men ...
In my mind, I've lived the scene in Sugar Hill way before Romello,
Way before you could explain why I'm so dark and you're so yellow.
Now a man, I understand skin tones and that being a different
complexion ...
Doesn't mean I'm less than.
In my darkest hour I feel you encouraging me to switch off my anger ...
Yes, ma'am!
Cowards pretend it's all a pump your chest thing
When the wisdom of your whispers made life for them an investment.
Strength is my intangible I never call on, but it's always there.
I wonder ... if it was your eternal sleep that made fear not as welcome
as steal, lie, and cheat?!
Drums make the stories in my head, walk on beat,
Successfully hiding my tears in plain sight, from what I have seen.
Arrogant as a child, I used to wonder ... why, when I'm mad at you, I
don't turn green?
Lost in thought ... I now see the measure—
Like, what's heavier, a thousand pounds of rocks, or a thousand pounds
of feathers?
Thirty-five years of you gone and my love gets no lesser,
Memories that once was now tend to get faded ...
So, every accomplishment, I whisper, "We made it," in celebration of you,
Beyond the walls of imprisonment that yearns to keep me jaded!

317

Rotten Nooses

It's like a tie that's too tight.
Grandma said, "It looks cute, but it's choking the life out of you!"
As you grow older, you begin to see it trying to take the fight out of you.
If your fingers could just pry it loose . . .
Psychologically, hugs become metaphoric nooses—deuces!!
But even that ties you to a deeper struggle,
No love, no one to hug you . . .
In rage, you scream: F you!
In protest, you fight for the very thing you hate,
Tattoos littered around your neck,
Scared to put a condom around your penis, craving shorty that's thick,
When you can't even count the times she's been on some clingy shhh!
Haze and liquor mixed—now it's around your eyes . . . Shit!
Blind blackouts, a chipped tooth from getting smacked out,
Remnants of remembrance as you rub your face like . . .
How the hell did I end up in a crack house?!
Tiny ropes choke and hang our conscience;
Unaware, you become addicted to the torture of rotten nooses
and nonsense.
The reason white folks made politics,
And now we blame them for not trying to reverse the effects of
treating us like objects.
What are you, a novice?
It's never the ropes that's rotten;
It's their souls, when slavery optics keep them watching,
Reliving a doctrine that psychologically made us hang ourselves . . .
I think, when they abolished slavery, we never took the time to
thank ourselves.

Suicidal Love

Just the taste of her cemented my longing.
Lost by the whiff of her perfume—
I found myself in awe and disgusted all at once,
Elongated as my manhood . . .
She stretched my imagination as far as the summer's edge.
The nights we fought . . .
I found myself rappelling down what ought to be a life of union,
Except, instead of a man grandma raised, I was a man in ruin.
Desolate visualizations as I searched the windows of her eyes for . . .
a we, an us, or a 4-ever
mine that I could not find.
As I search for meaning I've paced the floor in her empty footsteps
wondering . . .
What's next, what's best for me?!
Did she weep deceptively?
How could she leave me so unexpectedly?!
The feeling made my wrists feel like cutting boards!
Immediately, my breathing became faint—
As if my heart beat to the rhythm of a Barry White song,
My mind beginning to dance awkwardly as my blue blood liquified
the floor in red.
When I awoke from the deepest sleep I've taken in months,
I could hear the whispers of blurry people in white coats, possibly
prescribing me meds.
The eerie thing was . . .
There was no ache to my heart, nor no throb in my head;
No longer did I need the love I was chasing.
I thought to myself . . . Is my memory erasing?
Erratic, I began to scream for a love I could not remember.
As I rose, my body still somberly lying still, I froze . . . and I thought . . .

Hey! Where is my medicine?!
Just then a voice replied back . . .
Sorry—this is what happens when you let the devil win;
In love, and suicidal, I've released you as the devil's friend!

One Second of a Moment

It only takes one second to make a choice and learn that the world
is not as forgiving as you thought it was.
See . . . my seconds have been lined in blood
From fights to sights unpleasant . . .
Nights where my ego tells me, with one line I could be destined.
But for every second in my fifteen minutes of fame
It took only one second to cause me shame!
I choose not to let anger steal a spot in my mind.
'cause, see—my grind is predicated on the mastery of my time.
So, now, for each second that ticks . . .
A criminal thinking error loses its grip.
It only takes a couple of hard years to pick from the orchard that is me.
The fruit is my soul, my limbs are the tree.
I repeat . . . Something I said years ago:
It only takes one second to change the meaning of FREE!

Intracranial Warfare

Submerged in wisdom, in a place full of hate . . .
I remain foreign.
An immigrant to surroundings that are impossible to penetrate,
desolate beings cognitively congregate as I masturbate their minds
into submission . . .
Pause – before you get the wrong impression and Hercules my aggression!
I have a confession: this man that you perceive as a mere mortal . . . is
God, here to birth these lessons, I've burped these peasants . . .
You breathe mechanical ideologies as I manifest my philosophy.
Intellectual procreation reprises the fight in me, understanding defeat
is how the oppressors lie to me.
Lost but found, I'm questioning the articulation of the curriculum
they call our education that's provided for me!?
Doctored doctrines gives false pretenses;
They gave me this shovel and assumed I'd bury myself beneath the
trenches—beneath the black-robed henchmen, I see fear instead
of anger . . .
Unable to comprehend, so they wear cloaks to pose as strangers.
Consumed by danger woven into their DNA.
Yet, when I open my eyes . . .
I see killers become the prey, I see niggas niggardly eating for today,
hoping tomorrow will leave a lingering taste;
Ignorant to the fact that the damages of today, tomorrow just can't paste.
Which makes me think . . . was yesterday wasted on sour subliminals?
Or the deception of my art makes me a poorly trained criminal.
I prefer to think the consequences of my actions were minimal—
In hindsight, murder was preventable.
Victim of my environment, abducted lives are more than incidental . . .
Mentally chained, minorities are the majority, more than coincidental.
So in rage! We begin to vent too!!

Where's the Love

There's such a thing as friends and thugs,
but with gunfire the results only end in blood.
I'm from a place called ... Where's the Love!!
From birth I've been trained two ways, to love and survive.
But how can I if, every time I turn around, my understanding dies?!
I SHOUT: THE YOUTH IS OUR PRIDE!!!
I'm from a place called ... Where's the Love!! Don't cry, Where's
the Love, is it inside?
Nah ... inside prison is our pride, our joy, our little boy who's a
man now.
I'm from a place called ... Where's the Love!! Don't cry.
Why I shout! To love I'm devoted, optimistic I reign.
As a black brother, before I reign as a poet,
Where's the Love, I'm from that place and a friend asked how to
show it.
So I say unto you: Are you from Where's the Love?
No, not from Where's the Love, you pick up a gun and start blowing!
But from my hood, and every hood, where if you plant the seed, it
only starts growing.
STOP THE VIOLENCE

CONTRIBUTOR BIOS

Ahkivelli: Born in 1985, I was poured into the crucible containing the richness of hip-hop, from Cool G Rap to my favorite, Tupac Shakur. This was the closest tradition to poetry as I knew it. In 2016, I joined a creative writing program in prison. This program opened me up to a whole new world of poetry that I am still in love with to this day. As a result, I am now working on my degree in English Literature with the hope of offering to others what was offered to me—the opportunity to express/embrace different traditions of creative writing, such as Tupac, Sonia Sanchez, and Countee Cullen, as well as Shakespeare.

A lifelong Connecticut resident, **Kenneth Anderson** was born in 1963. He graduated from Central High school in 1981 and went on to Clinton to study theology. In 1982, he joined the US Navy and was accepted into the CT State Police Academy in 1989. However, unforeseen circumstances did not allow Kenneth to continue. He caught his first felony case and was headed on a downward spiral of crime. He ultimately robbed three banks in South Carolina, where he was sentenced to 15 years. Released in 1998, he later re-offended in CT and was sentenced to 10 years. He was released in 2015. While on the inside at Garner Correctional Institution, he took Chris Belden's creative writing class as well as Applied Theater with Garner librarian Mark Aldrich. Mr. Anderson continues working in theater and writing and has become effective in his church, where he was recently appointed the position of Elder. He has obtained his operation engineer card and currently works as a crane operator.

Lucky Barbera served eleven years in prison and was released in 2017. He worked as a tattoo artist until he lost his job due to the Covid-19 pandemic in 2020. So he started a mural business, painting large-scale work for both commercial and residential clients. In 2021, he opened his own tattoo studio, where he now works full time.

John L. Benjamin: If you combine the words "ambitious," "gifted," and "unique," that is as close as you'll get when describing me. I am 30 years old, from New Haven, CT, with five sisters and two brothers, with me being the youngest. I always had a love for writing, and throughout my life I've been fortunate to seize writing opportunities that presented themselves to me. I'm a certified chef apprentice and am currently in the process of getting a degree in real estate. One major goal I have is to get the chance for my words to be heard or read around the world, whether it be through reciting my poetry or the dialogue I put in a play or short story.

Christopher B. Berchem has struggled with anxiety and depression for most of his life. Poetry, math, and chemistry have helped him cope with these issues.

Ronald Bey: I was born in Chicago, Ill., on Feb. 6, 1976. I moved to Connecticut in the summer of '89. I've since then lived mostly in the towns of Bloomfield and Hartford. I now reside in Hartford, CT, with my wife of seven years, Victoria Bey.

John-Russell Bossé: I was born in Malden, MA, and brought up in neighboring Lynn. Since the age of six I have been diagnosed with mental illness, and since the age of fifteen have visited a number of psychiatric institutions. A nervous breakdown in 2001 sent me to prison for the first time. Throughout my life's turbulence, though, I have always had a gift for writing and storytelling. It was not until playwright/actor Beth Young and writer/educator Chris Belden volunteered to come to Garner CI to teach that I ever gave serious thought to systematically approaching this craft. Their patient instruction, as well as the discipline they helped to instill, allowed me to temper my skills. This refinement is an ever evolving and revealing journey that those two companions of spirit make with me every time I am blessed enough to take a pen to words. They are with me now as I write this, and I thank them for joining a luminous community of influential figures of my life. I hope that the skills they are helping me develop also make the world for others that much more worth living for and serving.

Juan Botello: I was 23 years old at the time "A View of Myself" was written. Now I'm 35 years old—and the journey continues . . .

Jamar Boyd: I am a resident of New Haven, CT. I am a 35-year-old man who has been incarcerated since the age of 17. I started off in the Applied Theater classes held at Garner C.I. with no prior experience, and my only skill set was as a rap artist. I am a good listener and can take direction if needed, and once I applied myself I was able to combine my rap performances with dramatic movements and scripts to entertain, educate, and inform my audiences, and I found great pride in the results. I have now started my own theater classes here at Osborn, C.I., with the facilitator/instructor Beth Young. Theater has changed my life for the better, and I can express myself in ways I once was never able to. I now look forward to movie scripts!

Solomon Boyd: I don't know what a bio really is—sounds like self-grandiosity. But anyway, I received my schooling in White Plains, NY, and Anchorage, AK, and attended Mercy College. My love for fiction inspires my passion for the arts, which was born as a child sitting on the living room floor watching TV. All good parents should let their children watch as much as they can (with good guidance, of course).

Nathaniel Boykin: No bio provided.

Lee Gary "Bear" Brewer was born prematurely on May 2, 1984, and grew to be a mountain of a man at 6'3" and 240 pounds. He was the baby of the family, with an older brother and two older sisters whom he loved and was very close to. Lee was raised by his mother and proud to be called a Mama's Boy. He was very athletic and participated in most outdoor sports, but was especially passionate about football. Lee played throughout high school as well as with the now defunct semi-pro Hartford Whales. Lee had a softer side that he showed in his love of art and poetry, spending hours honing his skills as a sketch artist and poet. His art was darkened by the demons of his heroin addiction, which can be seen in this collection of his works. Lee was barely eighteen when he fathered his son Danny, but even at that young age he was determined to better himself and defeat his demons and prove he could be a good role model,. But his demons were hard to overcome, and when he lost custody of Danny, he was left broken and in despair. It would take him seven years to take that hill in his battle against opioids, focusing on his education in Environmental Sciences. Lee was a loving gentle giant of a man with a boyish charm that could warm the coldest of hearts. He lived with passion each and every day. He lost that final battle in the war over his addiction on the morning of June 10, 2019, at the age of thirty-five. But for those who were fortunate enough to know him and were touched by him, they will fondly remember this giant Teddy Bear of a young man with the boyish grin, and their hearts will smile. (*Bio provided by Lee's mother.*)

John Brewer III: No bio provided.

Anthony (Nick) Brunetti: I'm 41 years old, born 11/23/80. Been incarcerated for 22 years, worked hard at rehabilitating myself, wrote a book called *A Lifer's Perspective*, and can read and write Hebrew. Also, an avid student of religious/spiritual studies.

Nathaniel O. Chambers: I received an honorable Discharge from the US Army as an E-5 Sergeant September 2014. My Military Occupational Specialty (MOS) was 56M "Chaplain's Assistant." I volunteered to deploy to Baghdad, Iraq, 2009-2010. The highlight of my time overseas was running the unit ministry team's religious services as well as becoming featured in Ride BMX UK's website for the B.O.B. Bikes Over Baghdad Tour. Being able to meet some of my heroes in the BMX Street, Park, and Flatland Professional community was life changing. Thanks for reading. God bless, stay humble, and support our service members.

Chey-Patron: I came from a mind that was limited to the perimeters of my environment. I'm no longer selling myself short and am evolving and growing in order to continue my unique story/journey toward a life worth living, demanding respect from people that see me as a resilient man, a man who values freedom, time, family, and life itself.

Veronica-May Clark is a 47-year-old transexual woman originally from Scotland. Since coming to prison in 2007, she has been creating art, mainly in ball point pen and also mixed media. In 2014, she started Prison Art Fights Children's Cancer, a charity that uses artwork created by prisoners in order to raise money to help children afflicted with cancer. Now in her sixth year of transition (not including the two years living full-time as herself before prison), she became the first person ever to initiate medical transition while in custody of the CT Dept. of Corrections. It took her a year and a half to receive any medical treatment, during which time she was continually denied treatment for her serious medical need and even resorted to self-treatment by way of self-surgical castration to alleviate

327

at least some of the dysphoria she had been experiencing most of her life. As of this writing, her legal battles continue.

I am **Filipe Colón**, an Original Man born in Boríquen on January 13, 1981, and my boys call me Cee-Lo. I am from Holyoke, MA, a small urban city full of flave and a large population of Boríquas. I am a live lover of Hip Hop music and writing. I write plays, poetry, and all my thoughts on real life situations. I am on my way home from doing a 20-year prison term with a new view on life, a positive one.

Born in Bridgeport, CT, **Exodus Cooke** was sentenced to 85 years in prison. For decades, his family, friends, and teachers told him he should become a writer, but he did not see what they all had noticed, and didn't take his writing of stories and poems seriously. That was the case until GOD answered his prayer and led him to participating in a creative writing class, where he witnessed great authors of storytelling and poetry be awed by his own poetry. Exodus continues to write. He will soon have two books coming to market. Both are a series of poems, one being *I Am My Neighbor, the Human Race*, the other *A Tribute to Her, to Him!* (Contact: Exodus Cooke #169077, 900 Highland Ave. Cheshire CT 06410)

Ian. T. Cooke was arrested in 2006, when he was eighteen years old, and has been continuously incarcerated since then. He is currently serving a "natural life" sentence but is hopeful to receive some form of vindication before that sentence is complete. While incarcerated, Ian has had the pleasure of meeting many gracious people, most of whom freely volunteered their time to inmates.

My name is **Robert Coover**, but all my friends call me **Moët**. I'm 38 years young and was born and raised in Bridgeport, CT. I am the proud father of one daughter. I've enjoyed writing since I was young.

For me, it's an escape. When I'm writing, I can be a knight, a doctor, a soldier, a father, even the President—I can be whatever I want to be in that moment. I appreciate everyone who took the time to get to know us and help us turn our imagination into reality.

Charles DeVorce: Born in Upstate New York and raised in Connecticut. I was always driven to write in some capacity or other—short stories, one- and two-act comedies, and especially poetry. Being a father and grandfather, I endeavor to write some things for this audience. With formal writing instruction on the horizon, could there be an audience waiting in the wings for this writer to emerge?

Ivan Diaz: I write from Suffield, CT. I like writing short inspirational pieces and stories. I'd describe myself as a word lover, and writing allows me to meld them to create literary art that informs, inspires, and gives readers a different view of the world around us. I am a former student of Mr. B and [Garner librarian] Mark Aldrich, both of whom taught, mentored, and enhanced my fondness for writing. I am honored to be included in this anthology and grateful for the opportunity to be heard by many readers. Thank you.

The Doves: Growing up in a drug-, gang-, and poverty-infested area wasn't easy. Especially when your mother has to play the role of your father as well. Watching her struggle to make ends meet, depressed, with a smile on her face makes you want to help by any means. But becoming a product of my environment caused more hurt than help to my mother. Sometimes situations occur in life, and you have to be able to think about the long-term effect rather than the instant gratification. Incarceration doesn't mean that your life is over, because as long as you're still breathing, change is possible, no matter the aspect (mental, physical, spiritual, etc.).

Norman Gaines: I have been incarcerated since I was 17 years old, and I'm currently 45 years of age. Before I began writing for Mr. Belden, I was not offered any programming because of my life-without-parole sentence. The work you have been given the chance to read here is due to Mr. B finding a way to convince the Department of Corrections to allow programming for men like me. This class helped me to enhance my skills to write and communicate my innermost thoughts as well as to open my mind to all different kinds of writing styles, views, and others' perceptions. I'd have you know this is the reason I'm on my way home and currently maintaining a 4.0 average for an associate's degree in Human Services.

Traveling around the world as an early teen allowed **Martin P. Gingras** to explore the world and see it from a new perspective. He uses this unique view on life to inspire him to use his words and create worlds for all walks of life. No matter the age, Martin's readers can explore the world he sees and experience it from his imagination. Martin's incarceration gave him the avenue to begin his writing.

Rasheen Giraud: No bio provided.

Mashawn Greene: I am 44 years old and enjoy writing as a way to ease my mind and share a piece of myself with others. I also enjoy reading the works of others as a way to better myself and learn different ways to express myself through my craft. Writing has been a peace for me, a silence in the middle of the storm. As I continue to grow through my writing, I also see my mental and spiritual growth as well. Writing has kept me grounded, and that allows me to stay in tune with what I love the most: my family. I will continue reading and growing, and I hope it shows in my writing. Peace and blessings.

The name is **Bryan Goodwin**, but most know me by Green Eyez. I'm 42 years old and from Bridgeport, CT, but I live in New Haven now. I've been writing for some years, but I never did nothing with my poems until the day I met this person by the name of Veronica-May Clark. She told me to write more and put myself out there, so I did—and look what happened. So, I want to say thank you to her, and I also want to say to Mr. Belden, thank you.

Joe Grosso was born in Connecticut, became addicted to opiates, and was incarcerated for robbery. He loves rock'n'roll, Hemingway, woodworking, Thai food, and snow. He hates mayo, ketchup, and mustard, as well as flavored water, prison, and hot weather. Joe thinks that everyone should listen to the Beatles and Elliot Smith; that everyone should read Virginia Woolf and Hemingway; and that everyone should try to be just a little bit kinder.

JV Harvey was born in Brooklyn, New York, and moved to Connecticut when he was ten years old. An award-winning independent filmmaker, his first love is Documentaries. His film *Room 306 MLK* has won seven independent awards. JV is also author of the self-published novel *A Step into The Rain* and two children's books, *Harvey The Little Brown Duck* and *Even Dragons Have To Go To Bed*. JV has written and sold more than ten screenplays and is currently working on another novel, *Seasons of Death,* and more children's books. Contact JV Harvey at jvhfilms@gmail.com

Isschar M. Howard is a forty-three-year-old man currently serving a life sentence in prison. He is an original mentor in the TRUE Program. He describes himself as a man who is on a path of redemption.

Israel: I was born in 1972 on March 14. I am a country boy, and nature is my one true home upon this earth. I love outdoor activities. I am

331

pursuing my BA in Religious Studies and hope to become a pastor, counselor, and friend to many who are hurting and lost.

Marquis Jackson was born in New Haven in 1979. He was arrested in 1999 for a murder he did not commit and was exonerated in 2018. While at the Garner Correctional Institution he was in a theater class from 2009-2018, writing, directing, and performing in many plays presented to an outside audience. In the creative writing workshop he wrote and performed his own poems and stories. He also worked in the library as a desk clerk and received the highest grade in his Culinary Arts Class.

Latone James was born in 1976 and raised by his mother and grandmother. He has been incarcerated since 1995. He married in 2015 and is the father of a 28-year-old daughter.

Kareem Leach: I am currently serving 14 years for assault in the first degree and robbery in the first degree. During the course of my incarceration, I've made the best use of the tools available in order to further my writing ability and express myself, my pains, and my joys through the art of poetry. Successes as well as failures come in waves; we just have to weather the storm.

Charles Logan: No bio provided.

Michael P. Mark, Jr. was born in Waterbury, CT. He is a graduate of the John F. Kennedy High School Class of 2006. He is the proud recipient of the 2021 St. Jude Children's Research Hospital Appreciation Award. He also completed the Blackstone Career Institute Paralegal Studies course with distinction. Michael is the author of *The Joy Behind Sorrow*, a collection of short poems filled with many different emotions. He was also a student at Quinnipiac University, where he studied crime and society, sociology, and sociology of economics. Of all his accomplishments, his proudest is his beautiful daughter, Michaela Mark.

Hunter McGinty: I made horrible choices in my past that put me in prison. Prison wasn't as bad as I thought it would be, though it was not a pleasant experience. I believe I have learned a lot about myself and have come to a better understanding about how life works and, most importantly, what's important in life: serving God as I understand Him.

Alexis "Lex" Melendez: I am 37 years old, from Manchester, CT. I am serving an 18-year sentence for Robbery and am a recent College Graduate, the first in my family. I have been incarcerated for half my life and have completed every program the D.O.C. has to offer. I wrote these writings in the darkest days of my life, but by telling my stories I got to bring closure, heal scars, let go of pain, and escape the reality of my cell!

Mount Yeti came to America to pursue his American Dream. He worked hard and authored or co-authored a few articles on diabetes, aging, and molecular biology of cancer in peer reviewed journals. He is a devoted son, brother, husband, and father and enjoys taking care of people in need. He was born in the South, a tropical Yeti, and from the Bible Belt. In 2008, he was falsely accused of threatening one of his coworkers and was fired from his job. In 2010, he was charged with murder. In 2017, New Haven Superior Court ordered forced medication based on a false diagnosis of schizophrenia. To avoid the permanent injuries caused by the paralyzing drug, he took a "plea bargain" and is currently serving time while waiting for a possible parole in the next five years.

Mystery (aka Mark Edwards): I am 39 years old. I love to write and express myself and the deeps thoughts I have. Writing comes from my heart, whether I'm reflecting on joy or pain. I have been incarcerated for 22 years and am currently on a new journey to make real friends. I've realized that good friends will empower you to be better. If you wish to connect with me on this journey, please contact me at MacDougal C.I. (1153 East St. South, Suffield CT, 06080).

D. Paschal (aka K. L. Paschal-Barros) is a Latinx and African American. He learned to read late in his education. From J.K. Rowling's *Harry Potter* books his world of language arts was unlocked. His primary career is culinary, but he also enjoys authoring his future books, from fantasy to nonfiction. His inspiration in life comes from his lover, Purple Raven.

Lawrence Perry: No bio provided.

Jose Luis Pesanté Jr was born beneath the bane of a South Bronx "barrio" to Milagros De Leon and José Pesante. Anchored in Connecticut with two sons, Jose L. Pesanté III and Jeremie Reyes, and "Papa G" to granddaughter Abiri. Grateful to have life and limb infused with the skills to transplant my journey into the vignettes of readers' minds.

Terrell Britton, AKA **Real Rell**, was born in Bridgeport, CT, and raised in Stratford, CT. Terrell always had a passion for art, especially music, poetry, and painting. Terrell is an artist himself—a songwriter, poet, and graphic designer. He also participates in community service as a way to give back to where he came from. He represents freedom, justice, and equality for all lives, and he also has family throughout Connecticut, where he currently resides.

Abdullah As Siddiq: Poetry has become a way for me to express myself openly. I came into prison at seventeen years old, and I was mad at the world. Poetry helped to curb my anger, and I was able to find myself. If it helped *me*, I know it can help others to grow and find themselves as well. Getting thoughts out on paper helps one to feel vulnerable and free. Any and everything is a form of poetry. Peace.

Quan Soyini: I'm a 46-year-old black man born and raised in the north end of Hartford, CT. I'm currently serving a life sentence at the Walker-MacDougall Correctional Institution, located in Suffield, CT. Everything I've done in my life thus far can't equal or overshadow my current situation. I am a has been. I used to be a brother, friend, uncle, lover, and father. I'm fighting for my life. That's all that matters at this time in my life: my life and liberty.

Michael Streater: D.O.B. 06-14-72, Brooklyn, NY. Youngest of seven, currently serving thirty years for First Degree Murder. Father of two daughters and grandfather of five children. Ardent lover of writing (sometimes ☺).

STYLUS: No bio provided.

Tall Eagle: My life has not been an easy one. From a very young age I've been in and out of mental hospitals, foster homes, boys' homes, detention centers, and other places as such. Until at last I am in prison until I die. What got me to this point would start from the times of abuse by my parents. Back when I was a child there were no laws to protect children. My greatest help came when I learned how to write poetry. By writing, I am able to put true feelings safely on paper without it being known how much of myself is in the words I write. A few years ago, I had my name legally changed to my Native American name: Wanblihanska Sungmanitu Mniinilaya. It is in

335

Lakotan and means Tall Eagle, Coyote, Silent Water. I myself am Apache and Blackfoot. As a child I was robbed of my language, but I am now able to speak some Lakotan, and I honor them.

Jenkins Tarlue: No bio provided.

I, **Terrance D. Thompson**, 52, am a lifelong resident of New Haven, CT. Due to several bad decisions, I became an inmate housed at Garner Correctional Institution. There, I enrolled in a creative writing course and had the extreme pleasure of working with Mr. Chris Belden, who helped me to learn about other modes of poetry and sparked an interest to share my work!

Andy M.T. was born May 20, 1987, in Hartford Hospital and grew up in Bristol, CT. He was active in the Cub Scouts and Boy Scouts and started working at age 12 as a newspaper delivery boy. He attended E.C. Goodwin Tech High School and Johnson & Wales University. In 2011, Andy hiked the Appalachian Trail from Georgia to Maine. He was released from prison in 2019 after serving three years.

Vaughn Walker (aka Legend, aka Biggz Diablo): I've been writing lyrics and poetry for years, and it's been very therapeutic. It's allowed me to grow from a boy to a man through my adversity and to express myself in a way that I can give back to other young writers. It's also allowed me to pay forward the talent I believe was God-given. I hope my words touch readers in the way that it soothes their soul and allows me to express the king in me to other young royals looking to be great. Peace and love.

Patrick Walsh was born in New Britain, CT, and raised in Colchester and Lebanon, CT, before moving back to New Britain in his early teens. He attended Unity College in Maine and Central Connecticut

State University. Patrick was a paid Firefighter for the City of Bristol and a Tattoo Studio owner and operator. He has been incarcerated since 1995. A trial in 1998 concluded with a hung jury. In 1999, prosecutors overstepped their authority and Patrick was wrongfully convicted of murder. He was sentenced as a "virtual" lifer (55 years to serve, without early release options such as parole or good time). He continues to appeal his conviction. Patrick is a loving father and adored grandfather of five grandchildren. His writings printed herein are mostly based on true life events, though names have been changed.

Chauncey Watts: As a child growing up in an urban environment such as Hartford, CT, life had many challenges. My parents' domestic disputes and drug abuse had a profound effect on me. At the age of ten, I came to the conclusion that tranquility and peace existed outside of my home environment, and I decided to stay away as much as possible. When I turned eleven, I was introduced to marijuana and alcohol by adults in the neighborhood who thought it would be amusing to see an eleven-year-old boy getting high. At thirteen, my mother informed me that my only father figure was not my actual biological father. Then I was introduced to a stranger who was battling drug addiction, which allowed no room for love or support. Two years later, my now-stepfather's and mother's recreational cocaine use advanced to crack cocaine. Poverty and turmoil came immediately. The streets and other adults became my primary source of guidance, which resulted in me selling the same poison that was destroying my household. A year later, at fifteen, I felt I was a man. The influence of alcohol and marijuana, along with a few pennies in my pocket, gave me the illusion of stability and independence. At seventeen, I developed friendships with those similarly situated and equally lost. As a result, I became a part of a subculture where practical decision making was replaced with the desire for love and acceptance. Although my life had many struggles, I refuse to make excuses for the harm I have caused. This reality, consolidated with remorse, gives me hope that one day I can help youth and young adults at risk avoid getting involved in gangs, crime, and violence, which ultimately create victims. If my life experience or that of others can save one person and help them avoid such obstacles, then we are all one step closer to creating a positive legacy.

Max Well: I had, and have again, a spiritual life. I spent two years in prison, which was hell except for some classes and lots of book reading and family and friends both in and out of prison. I've been a recovering addict for years and have written poetry and short stories on and off. But in prison I was given guidance in a poetry class run by Mr. Belden. It was the highlight of my week, and I took the assignments to heart, and they made me a better writer.

Rocky Williams of Hartford, CT, known as **The Illestrator** [sic], has been writing for 28 years. He has written poetry and hip-hop from an "on the scene" perspective, and illustrates pictures with colorful vividness, evoking raw emotion from readers and listeners alike.

ACKNOWLEDGEMENTS

Thank you to everyone at Woodhall Press: Colin Hosten, David LeGere, Miranda Heyman, and especially my editor Christopher Madden. Your support and enthusiasm for this project has been inspiring.

Special thanks to all those who supported my work at Garner Correctional Institution, including Deputy Warden Kim Jones, Counselor Bonnie Hakins, and Warden Scott Semple. Extra thanks to former Garner librarian Mark Aldrich, who showed me the ropes.

Big thanks to the folks at the Westport Writers Workshop who helped fund several editions of *Sentences*.

Eternal gratitude goes out to my wife, Melissa DeMeo, and my daughter, Frankie Belden, for not objecting to their husband and father walking into a maximum-security prison each week for more than ten years.

Finally, thanks to the incarcerated writers I worked with over so many years. Your grit, courage, and talent will forever amaze me.

ABOUT THE EDITOR

Chris Belden is the author of two novels, *Carry-on* and *Shriver* (basis for the film *A Little White Lie*), and the story collection *The Floating Lady of Lake Tawaba*. His essay "Inside Words: How to Teach Writing in Prison" won the 2013 Bechtel Award from Teachers & Writers Magazine. A 2019 Connecticut Arts hero and graduate of the Fairfield University MFA Program, Chris is an instructor at the Westport Writers Workshop.

Portrait by Ian T. Cooke